Retirement Rules

3 Steps for Planning Your New Financial Future

Retirement Rules

3 Steps for Planning Your New Financial Future

Matthew J. Dicken

Published by Author Academy Elite
P.O. Box 43
Powell, Ohio 43065
www.AuthorAcademyElite.com

Printed in the United States of America.

ISBN: Paperback: 978-1-64746-049-5
Hardback: 978-1-64746-050-1
Ebook: 978-1-64746-051-8
LCCN: 2019919189

Note to the Reader:

Most people say they want a better understanding of their retirement finances. Yet, these same people invest more time planning their annual vacation than designing their roadmap to retirement. This is because the complexities of the financial services world and the fear of making the wrong decisions often paralyzes us. Since founding Strategic Wealth Designers in 2002, we've helped thousands of clients overcome their fears and build a successful plan for a fun and exciting retirement. In this updated and expanded edition of *Retirement Planning in a New Direction*, you'll understand:

- The myths of diversification and how to avoid fees that chip away at your nest egg.
- Why tax planning is so important when it comes to your Social Security.
- The critical difference between the accumulation and distribution phases of retirement saving.
- And much more.

Get ready to discover the 3 steps for planning your financial future.

—Matt Dicken, founder of Strategic Wealth Designers

NOTE TO THE READER

[illegible]

- [illegible]
- [illegible]
- The [illegible] and [illegible]
- And much more.

[illegible]

[illegible]

Table of Contents

Rule Three: Keep it Simple

Getting Started

Introduction

Three Rules for a Prosperous Retirement

I knew that something must be different about how the families of two of my buddies handled their money. But to my twelve-year-old mind, it didn't make sense: Both dads had similar jobs at the same company. Neither mom had a paying job. Yet one family always seemed to be in a financial crunch, and the other seemed relaxed and ready for anything. "What's going on?" I asked my parents one day. "At Tom's house, they're always arguing about money, even if it's just for a pair of shoes or to get the car fixed. But at Jim's house, there's enough for all that and a lot of fun stuff too."

"Well, Jim's family probably budgets, plans, and saves," my dad told me, "and Tom's family maybe just spends everything and doesn't set anything aside for emergencies, so when something goes wrong they don't have any money for that."

I went to my room and thought about that awhile. An hour or two later I came back and sat down with my parents at the kitchen table.

"I have it figured out," I told them. "I'm going to help Tom's folks. See, they can send me their paycheck, and I'm going to give them an allowance. Then I'll pay all their bills for them, but I'll also make sure I set some aside for savings—and

I'm thinking I could charge them something to keep doing that for them."

My mom smiled at me. "Well, Matt, I don't think anybody's going to turn over their finances to a twelve-year-old." But my parents told me that what I was describing sounded a lot like what a financial planner would do.

"Really?" I said. "Okay! That's what I'm going to do when I grow up, because I want to help people. I want to help them be smart with their money."

"THIS IS OUR NEW CHIEF FINANCIAL OFFICER."

From that moment, everything that I did was geared toward becoming a financial planner. I still had fun as a kid, but on rainy days I'd turn on the financial news, read investing books, or study the history of the markets and the economy.

In high school I was active in Future Business Leaders of America and Junior Achievement and was a Stock Market

Game winner. I received numerous national awards and, at age eighteen, caught the attention of financial institutions that could see where I was heading. A major one offered me an internship—quite a jump start.

I entered the industry in 1997 and by 2002 had started my own firm, Strategic Wealth Designers. As you will recall, in 1997 it seemed like anyone could throw darts to choose stocks and get 20 or 25 percent returns. Investors started to believe they could count on such returns every year. If you were getting 15 percent returns, you may have felt like firing your advisor.

Because I had studied market history, I knew that it wasn't going to go up forever. Even then I was advising investors to keep a portion of their money in a safer position. Many didn't listen, but quite a few did.

Then, from 2000 to 2002, stock market investors were losing 30 to 50 percent of their account values. My clients did very well. If they had any losses at all back then, they were very small, because we had them in a safer position. Not all their money was at risk in the market.

Meanwhile others were telling me that the market plunge had put their retirement dreams on hold. They had to go back to work, downsize their homes. I met people going into retirement with 80 to 100 percent of their retirement assets tied up in the stock market—often in technology funds or small-cap funds. They were failing to have a successful retirement not because the market had corrected but because they carried too much risk in their portfolios. So close to retirement, they never should've had their money invested entirely in the stock market.

A lot of financial advisors closed up shop in those days. The downturn flushed them out, and many went into the mortgage industry. They found another bubble. I don't know where they've landed at this point. But as they were struggling, my business was thriving. We had clients who had little to no losses during that period. They were telling their friends, their coworkers and their family members about us and the work that we did.

A Safer Money Approach

I founded Strategic Wealth Designers so that I wouldn't be tied to a large company with quotas to meet. I could be independent and just do what was in the best interest of the client. I decided to focus on retirees and those who would be retiring within ten years.

At that stage of your life, taking a safer money approach makes a lot of sense. You don't carry as much risk but still can get a reasonable rate of return on your money. It's not good enough to just keep your money safe from market downfalls. You need a return that will keep up with inflation and outpace it so that you can take withdrawals.

Our core philosophy at Strategic Wealth Designers is to take a responsible approach to investing. We don't want clients to be afraid they will lose their money, but they still need to see it grow at a reasonable rate. We don't want you to make speculative investments unless you can afford to do so. We focus on investing a portion of our clients' assets in products that relieve them of the worry that they will go down in value—investments with a guaranteed, insured return. That's what most people should be looking for when they enter retirement.

Before starting my company, I worked for a major financial services firm but I wasn't in a traditional wire house doing a lot of churning and trading. The emphasis right from the beginning was on safety and insured accounts.

We have no interest in selling somebody a financial product and moving on. We take a holistic approach. We want to look at the overall plan and make sure the client is protected, whether from taxes, fees, excessive market risk or the financial strain of health issues that he or she may encounter. We want to make sure that the client's retirement will be financially bulletproof, with a lifelong income no matter what happens in the economy.

Most of our clients are fifty-five to seventy-five, from diverse backgrounds. Truck drivers. Doctors. A rocket scientist. An Olympic gold medalist. We have never set any minimum acceptable account size. If we can help somebody and provide value, that's what we want to do. If a client has $200,000 to retire on, that is just as important to him or her as $2,000,000 is to another client. Neither wants to run out of money. They need an income, and they want to be able to pass whatever is left to their spouses or their kids or grandkids when they leave this world.

We want clients whose investments feel significant to them. If someone walks through our door who has a nest egg of $100,000 and wants to invest $80,000 through us, that's significant to that person. That's a large portion of their liquid net worth. If someone has assets of $5,000,000 and wants to invest $100,000, we're going to decline. Obviously that client is not dealing with us as a trusted advisor who can guide him toward a successful retirement. He considers us to be more like a salesperson or a vendor who's there to solve a problem or provide a product. We don't want those relationships. We want to be a trusted advisor.

Clients with whom we work best are typically those who are tired of watching their nest eggs go up and down with the market. This is the advice they've been hearing, "Just sit tight. Ride it out. In the long run, the market always produces a strong return." That strategy is inappropriate for those contemplating retirement, yet advisors still tell them to put most of their nest egg in the market, diversify it, and see what happens. "You've got a long time horizon," they say. "You're going to be retired for a long time, so don't get caught up by the short-term corrections or bumps in the road. You'll be okay over the long term."

Of course, all the statistics say quite the contrary. If you try to just ride it out, and you're not proactive and working with an advisor who is an expert at retirement planning, then you will more than likely fail to have a successful retirement—which is defined by being able to maintain your standard of living up to your full life expectancy. Statistics show that most retirees have to drastically cut back their standard of living. In some cases they have to go back to work after they've been retired for several years. That may be because their advisors told them to wait out a down market and that their diversified mutual fund portfolios in the end would be just fine, that they had nothing to worry about. What they really were saying was that it was time to get a second opinion.

Don't let someone tell you to sit tight as your retirement savings go down the drain—especially when that someone is doing quite well by collecting fees from you. You need to be aware of the fees and taxes you must pay with certain investment options. Ask your advisor to break them all down for you. When we review mutual funds for clients in my office, we see annual fees, account fees, management fees, trading costs, wrap fees, inactivity fees, and low balance fees, among many others. You pay those fees whether or not your account is making money—and they can seriously diminish the chances for a safe retirement.

THREE SIMPLE RULES

1. ***Safety First***
2. ***Reasonable Return***
3. ***Simple***

Three Simple Rules

Our philosophy and practice are based on three financial rules, which this book will discuss in detail. They are: Safety comes first, get a reasonable return, and keep it simple. These governing principles will be an enormous help as you plan for retirement. If you stick to them, you could be well on your way to securing your financial future.

When clients ask for our help, these are the principles we agree upon. We reassure them they won't lose money in risky investments and that they nonetheless will get a reasonable return. And we're going to keep it simple and easy for them to understand. If the economy is doing well, they're going to make money. If the economy is doing poorly, they won't lose a lot of money. And that's about as complex as it gets.

Our clients can think of us as the pilot of a plane. They don't need to come into the cockpit and study every dial and gauge. They don't need to learn the flight manual. They can trust us to get to the destination safely; if they don't, we're not the pilot for them. Likewise, we don't fill clients' heads with complex financial jargon. We're happy to answer questions, but teaching clients how to fly isn't what we do. We guide them. We give them enough information so they understand exactly what's happening with their money. Most people just want to know they'll get safely to their destination with a smooth landing.

A Passion to Educate

Our true passion—and we don't consider what we do to be work—is educating the public on ways to retire successfully. Most people are following advice that is not going to work for them. It might work temporarily, but along comes a bear market or hyperinflation and retirement dreams fade.

We've met many people over the years who we couldn't help. They've done all the things we warn people not to do in our classes, educational events, and news appearances. Following a broker's bad advice, taking risk with their investments as though they're still in their twenties with decades to recover from a bear market. Withdrawing income from plunging accounts, paying exorbitant fees and taxes on their investments—all hastening their downward spiral towards a destroyed retirement.

Everyone knows someone like this. They may owe more on their house than it's worth. Perhaps somebody persuaded them to get a home equity line of credit and put that money into investments. These people are desperate. They don't have the resources and income for a successful retirement, and they want us to fix it. But there's no magic wand. We must tell them there is nothing that we can do. It's too late. The damage was done over the last ten to fifteen years. They have some very difficult decisions to make. They have to cut their standard of living, sell their house, perhaps move in with the kids. It's frustrating.

There's no reset button in your retirement. There's no do-over. You get one shot at getting it right. We want to prevent as many people as we can from finding themselves in such dire situations. It does not have to be that way. That's why we continue to do what we do. We can't help everybody, but we're going to help as many people as we possibly can have a successful retirement. The statistics show that 65 percent of retirees won't have enough to maintain their standard of living for the rest of their lives. That means two out of three people are getting it wrong. We want you to be part of that minority that succeeds.

RULE ONE

Safety Comes First

CHAPTER 1

TIME FOR A NEW APPROACH

Retirement means different things to different people. I'll meet with some people who will tell me, "Matt, when we were working, we sacrificed, sent the kids to college, saved everything that we could. So now we want to travel the world." Others tell me, "Matt, I don't have to go anywhere; I'll be happy if I don't have to get up for work Monday mornings."

The common denominator among retirees is they don't want to worry about their money. They don't want to worry where the next income check will come from. They just want to know they can rely on it being there. Whether they want a basic retirement or an extravagant one, they want money to be the least of their concerns.

Some people are very busy in retirement, and they're in a rush to do things that they've dreamed about doing. When our clients are in their sixties and seventies, they are the most active. They travel, visiting their kids and grandkids out of state, or going overseas.

But when retirees get into their eighties and nineties, the grandkids come to them. Older retirees are less likely to need as much money on a day-to-day basis. But after twenty years of retirement, the effects of inflation can start to show on their nest eggs. Things inevitably will cost more.

And how they spend their money is sure to change. They've seen as much of the world as they want to see, so vacation spending is less. But they're dealing increasingly with health issues and other concerns. The nature of spending transitions from the enjoyment of life to the sustaining of life, from a financial as well as a health perspective. Health-care spending goes up, and as retirees age they become concerned that the need for long-term care could swallow all their money.

This is also the time of life when people really think about their legacy. What do they want to be remembered for? Who should get their inheritance? Which charities will they endow? Their focus changes from "what are we going to do next week?" to "what are people going to say about us when we're gone?" During their retirement, people think increasingly about posterity and the mark they're going to make on the world.

A Change in the Rules

But the rules have changed in retirement. You might think you're going to be sitting on a porch in a rocking chair, but you're busier than ever. And you have new concerns—health concerns, issues with family and grandchildren. The rules of life have changed. But no one is giving you a new rule book.

The investment rules have changed as well. Too many retirees treat their money as if they still had another twenty or thirty years to go before retiring. They don't change the strategies they used in their twenties and thirties. And it just doesn't work.

As you get older the strategy has to change. You need a new approach to how you view your money. In your working years, you focused on growing your nest egg as large as possible. If you lost some money, you figured you had plenty of time to adjust and recover. But once you retire, that's it.

Your nest egg has a lot of pressure on it. It has to provide an immediate income. If you pass away, it has to be there for the surviving spouse—and statistically, a wife outlives her husband by twelve years. And many people hope to leave much of that nest egg to their children, and grandchildren, and charitable causes.

The pressure could remain on your nest egg for twenty or thirty years or beyond, depending on how long you live. I have a couple of clients whose mothers are 104 and 106 years old. They didn't plan for a forty-year retirement, but that's what happened. And my clients with aging parents are deeply concerned about making sure the money lasts as long as they do.

In retirement, you no longer have that luxury of time. There's no longer the option of saving more money. What you've got is what must see you through. It's what you will depend upon to reach your goals.

ACCUMULATION VS. DISTRIBUTION

Retirees need to acknowledge that they have moved to a different phase of their financial lives. During their working years, they were in the accumulation phase, in which they were investing and growing their assets for the future, without tapping them for expenses. Now, in retirement, they are in the distribution phase. Rather than putting money into accounts, you are looking to take money out. And that's why moving the money into a safe type of investment is so crucial.

However, most advisors focus on the accumulation phase, even for retirees—not recognizing that a fundamental shift in strategy is due. A retiree needs an advisor who focuses on the distribution phase.

Often retirees take more risk with their money than they should because they are trying to make up for something. They may be trying to overcome a market downturn that eroded their portfolio, for example—or a business failure, health issue, or divorce that did likewise. But taking additional risk thinking it will allow you to meet your retirement goals is incredibly risky and foolish. It is sure to worsen financial worries.

The first question I ask my clients is, "What is your number one financial concern?" Typically, they respond that they are worried they will run out of money during retirement. They're afraid they don't have a sufficient nest egg. And that's a valid concern. Most people don't. A 2018 study by the Center for Retirement Research found between 42 percent and 60 percent of U.S. households are at risk of not having enough money to make ends meet during retirement -- even if they cut their spending back to just 75 percent of preretirement levels. That means for every ten people you see on the street, as many as six are not prepared for retirement—or they're already retired and running out of money.

> WHAT IS YOUR NUMBER ONE FINANCIAL CONCERN

In many financial planning surveys, respondents are asked, "What is the number one thing you want your money to provide?" Almost always, they answer "security." If that is what they expect their money to provide—and their top fear is running out of it—why then do so many retirees have most, or all, of their assets tied up in the stock market? I meet them all the time—people in their fifties, sixties, and even eighties who have as much risk in their portfolios as young adults. Along comes a market crash—and you can be sure we'll see it happen again—and they cannot recover. Time is against them.

A well-known and very helpful rule of thumb is called the Rule of 100. It's a very simple method used to determine how much of your retirement assets you should have in equities or stocks and how much you should have in non-risk, safe alternatives. It works like this: Subtract your age from one hundred. The result is the percentage of your money that should be invested in stocks or equities, where it is exposed to risk. For example, if you are sixty years old, according to the Rule of 100, you should have no more than 40 percent of your portfolio at risk. If you're thirty, you can afford to have 70 percent of your assets exposed to risk, because you have time to make up for losses.

THE RULE OF 100

100
- 60 (Your Age)
40% at risk

Of course, every situation is different. The decisions you make are going to depend on your time horizon, your age, how close you are to retirement, and how much risk you want to have in your portfolio. If you're more risk-averse, you may want less exposure to the market than the Rule of 100 would suggest. If you'd like a little more risk, then you would put more of your assets in riskier investments. It's up to you, of course, but the Rule of 100 is a great benchmark.

THE THREE WORLDS OF INVESTMENT

The Bank World

You typically won't face risk with a bank's investment recommendations, but the returns will be very low. If you invest your money in CDs or money market accounts or savings accounts, you have found a way to lose your money safely. Inflation will surely lead you to loss. Not long ago the average one-year CD was paying about 1 percent interest, with inflation running at just under 3 percent. You can see how your money eventually will disappear—even in a so-called safe investment. Stuffing your money in a mason jar and burying it in the backyard could seem a better option.

However, bank instruments such as CDs remain popular because many people are risk-averse and want to avoid the emotional stress of volatility from the stock market. There's nothing wrong with having money in a CD, but you don't want to focus your retirement funds or IRA investments in CDs. Instead, you want to use your CD for emergency funds. That's really how it is designed to be used.

You also have some volatility even in a CD or savings-account type of instrument, as far as how much income you can expect. For example, say you have $1,000,000 in a retirement account and you want to live on the interest that it is generating. Typically, you could take somewhere between $10,000 and $30,000 per year over a twenty- or thirty-year retirement and be safely positioned—if that's all the income you needed from the account. Recently, however, the income would have been more like $10,000—and if your retirement plan called for more, you would fall short.

So in the investment world of the banks, you're not going to lose money because the market crashed or the economy tanked—but inflation, over time, is going to eat away at those dollars.

The Wall Street World

Most people invest the Wall Street way. The stock market exposes them to high risk, but they also have growth potential. If you have ever had money in a 401(k) or similar plan, you probably had some money tied to the stock market. Most investment marketing is targeted at the Wall Street way. The mutual fund industry alone, not counting big brokerage firms, spends about ten billion dollars per year on marketing and advertising.

When you do things Wall Street's way, you have to deal with the emotional stress of volatility. If you look at a chart of historic cycles in the U.S. stock market, you will see periods of sixteen or eighteen years in which there was little or no growth. In such periods, some years look good and others not so good, with the net result being nothing to show for it—and plenty of stress and volatility along the way. Inflation in those years is often higher than what the stock market returned.

As a Wall Street investor, you basically have to assume the responsibility of a pension manager. If you are fortunate enough to have a pension, you know you're going to get a guaranteed check every month. You don't have to worry about it. Somebody else, while you are working and while you're retired, has been investing the money for you, acting as steward of the money and making sure there's enough to last, hopefully, as long as you do. But when you invest the Wall Street way, you become the pension manager. You might have a financial advisor, but ultimately what happens with your investments is your responsibility. If you follow bad advice, it's you who suffers the consequences. All the risk is on your shoulders. And if we face another September 11 or 2008, your retirement savings will suffer grievously, and you won't have time to recover.

There's a myth that keeps people coming back for more, and that is the idea that Wall Street, over any ten-year period, averages an annual return of about 10 percent. Simply untrue. If you look at the actual returns, there have indeed been some ten-year periods where the market did that well, but there have been others where it didn't do anywhere near that. And if you look at the whole history of the stock market, the average returns have actually been quite a bit lower—only 5 percent, according to one analysis. And people who buy and sell frequently, more often than not, end up buying high and selling low, which can lead to getting significantly less than that. Why would you assume the risk that the stock market exposes to your portfolio just to get a 3 or 4 percent return, or even the average 5 percent? You could end up with a huge loss. If you are within ten years of retirement or already there, you don't have time to ride it out.

The statistics are clear: If you leave the majority of your money at risk in the stock market, you have to get pretty lucky in order to have a successful retirement. If you have $1,000,000 and you're relying on the stock market to provide your retirement income, expect that $40,000 to $50,000 per year is all that you will be able to draw out. AARP recently reaffirmed that individuals shouldn't withdraw any more than 4 percent from their retirement accounts based in the stock market.

The Hybrid World

Hybrid investing is a safer environment for your retirement dollars, and a retiree with a $1,000,000 portfolio can expect an income of $60,000 to $80,000 per year. Compare that with the $10- 30,000 per year from bank investments and the $40-50,000 per year from Wall Street.

That's what we define as a reasonable return. You need to earn 6 to 10 percent per year, on average, to have a successful retirement. If you're taking 5 or 6 percent out of the account each year, in some cases more, you need to be able to let a little of the earnings stay in the account in order to counteract the effects of inflation. Whatever you're earning, you don't want to take all of it out every single year, because eventually inflation will eat into your spendable dollars.

One of the most popular hybrid accounts is an indexed annuity. With the indexed annuity, you get the best of the bank world and the best of the Wall Street world. You have growth potential, but you don't have the risk that stock market poses. With some of the hybrid options, you have a safety net sitting under your money so your account cannot go down in value. Indexed annuities are popular among retirees or those who soon will retire, and that's really because these types of accounts are the only type of vehicles that can guarantee your principal AND a stream of income for the rest of one's life. Surveys show people are more concerned about running out of money prematurely than about dying prematurely. Yet some people are skeptical that hybrid investments could work for them. "Could I really get into a financial retirement strategy," they ask, "that will guarantee me income for the rest of my life?" The hybrid alternative seems like a foreign concept. They think they have to invest in the market to get ahead, or else put their money in the bank and accept whatever little interest is available.

We want to do better for your retirement plan and deal with investments that we know are going to be insured and guaranteed not to lose money but still have the opportunity for growth. Some types of annuities have been around for hundreds of years. It's not a new concept. In the hybrid world, instead of being your own pension manager and hoping you will pick the right investments, you can transfer the responsibility of the pension management to an insurance company. You take the risk off your shoulders—and gain the potential for a return that is 50 percent greater each year than you would get through a bank investment. There's also a significant difference in what happens to your principal. You can have more money to spend, to enjoy, and more to pass on to your heirs and beneficiaries.

Let's review. If you have $1,000,000 in CDs and you're getting 1 percent interest, chances are you're spending down your principal. Most retirees cannot live on $10,000 per year. If you invest your million dollars the Wall Street way and a market crash turns your portfolio into $700,000, there isn't any income to draw. You lost money, and if you have to draw an income, you're eating principal.

But with hybrid investing, in most cases the million dollars that you have in the account will still be there to pass onto your heirs or beneficiaries, or to counteract inflation. If you live to be one-hundred and twenty-five years old, it's going to be there for you. In the hybrid world, you can have guarantees that will last as long as you do. That's why hybrids are becoming so popular.

The banks and Wall Street don't necessarily want you to know about some of these options because they are not as profitable for them, but more and more people are finding out for themselves. Millions of Americans have some or all of their retirement assets in hybrid accounts, and they have been enjoying successful retirements even in difficult economic times. In the years to come, you're going to hear a lot more about the hybrid world of investments.

Active vs. Dormant Accounts

Historically when we go through a bear market, the average decline is 30.4 percent. That means $1,000,000 could turn into less than $700,000 if you have it all at risk. And if you're taking money out of the account, your portfolio cannot recover even if the market does. You've spent the money that would have rebounded.

Let's say your lifestyle needs require you to take out 5 percent annually, or $50,000. If you continue to do so when your account total has plummeted, the amount of your withdrawal can never go back up in value. It's gone. You don't recover from that type of scenario. That's why it is so risky to depend on an account that fluctuates with the markets to provide you with retirement income.

Some accounts are active, and others are dormant. In an active account, such as a 401k, 403b or IRA, you're still buying assets and contributing regularly. When the stock market goes down in value, you don't worry excessively because you're still buying shares, and you get them at lower cost. You will recover more quickly when the market goes up. Buying mutual fund shares regularly in an active account can be appropriate for some investors, because you take advantage of the volatility.

You want to avoid mutual funds in a dormant account, however. A dormant account is any account that you are not putting money into on a monthly basis; or even worse, an account from which you are withdrawing money. When the stock market goes down in value, you are going to lose money and you will not be using the volatility to your advantage. Instead you have to wait and hope that the market recovers.

There is a time and place to use mutual funds. But we meet with people every day who have dormant accounts that are 80 or 100 percent invested in mutual funds. It's a scenario that isn't working well for them. Over the last ten years it hasn't been a good approach, nor do we see it as an appropriate strategy for the next decade.

You could think of dormant and active accounts this way: If you have one dollar invested in a stock market index and the market crashes, losing 50 percent of its value, your dollar will be worth fifty cents. If you sit tight and the next year the market rallies, gaining 50 percent, do you have your dollar back? No, you have seventy-five cents. You'd have to have a return of 100 percent to offset the 50 percent loss.

Consistency Counts

Consistency is what counts when you're retired—not the wild swings up and down. It's like the tortoise and hare analogy. If you get a 10 percent average return on your money, that can actually outperform a 25 percent average return. Let me go over an example of how it works:

$100k + 100%	
vs.	$100k +10%
$200k -50%	$110k +10%
$100k	$121k

Let's say that you put $100,000 in a risky investment—perhaps someone convinced you that in the long run you would be fine. The first year it works well for you: You choose the right IPO or technology stock and get a 100 percent return. You now have $200,000. You're happy, so you do it again, and in the second year, because of a market correction, you lose half the account value. You're back to $100,000. It went up 100 percent, then it went down 50 percent. The industry considers that an average return of 25 percent over the two-year period—but in reality, you know you haven't gained a cent. And when you enter fees into the equation, it makes the situation even worse.

Now let's say that you don't want to take a whole lot of risk, and you look for more consistency. So you put your $100,000 into an account, and the first year you get a 10 percent return. Your $100,000 is now $110,000. The second year you invest the same way and get another 10 percent return. You now have $121,000. The average advertised rate of return on that investment is 10 percent. The other accounts advertised average rate of return is 25 percent, but the account that averaged 10 percent is worth more money.

It's the volatility, therefore, that can destroy a retirement. You need consistent, predictable, guaranteed results when the account must support your lifestyle for the next ten or twenty or thirty years. It's all really very simple math. It's the way that the numbers shape up through consistent returns year after year after year. It's a wise strategy that can bring you a worry-free retirement.

CHAPTER 2

WHAT THE STOCKBROKERS TELL US

Financial advisors and stockbrokers have us convinced that if we want a higher return on our money, we have to take more risk with it. Everyone has probably heard this at some point. But if you are going to take risk with your money, how do you keep it safe? Usually what they'll say is, "Don't put all your eggs in one basket. You need to diversify."

They usually recommend that you diversify with a portfolio of different mutual funds. But does owning mutual funds automatically keep your money safe? No, it doesn't. It wasn't safe in the last bear market, and it won't be in the next. So here is one of first the things you can do to secure your financial future: If your financial advisor is telling you that you will be just fine with your mutual funds, find somebody else.

A stock brokerage firm typically is not doing any long-term planning, specifically. The broker is looking to offer the hot stock of the week, or to get a bonus from peddling a mutual fund with which the firm has a selling agreement. It's a trader's mentality—buy a stock, sell it soon for a profit. They don't really consider the fees and tax implications. Not to mention what happens to your retirement plans if they are wrong and the stock goes down in value.

Those who work at wire houses typically have quotas. They have to sell, regardless of whether it's good for the client. They have to sell a certain amount of stock or a certain amount of a mutual fund, because that's what they're told they must do. When you work with an advisor of a stock brokerage firm or a bank, typically that person will be a registered representative. Their fiduciary responsibility is to their employer. Their responsibility is only to sell and recommend things to their clients that are suitable—not necessarily in their best interest.

Strategic Wealth Designers operates as a Registered Investment Advisor, which means we have a fiduciary responsibility to the client. We must do what's in the best interest of the client or risk being fined, losing our licenses or even going to prison. By contrast, a registered representative of a Wall Street firm, wire house or bank need only prove their recommendation was suitable.

The Myth of Diversifying

Warren Buffett once commented that when advisors recommend that you diversify, what they're really doing is trying to protect you from their own ignorance. If they really knew what was going on in the economy, and where the right place was to put your money, they would not recommend that you diversify. They would point you in the specific direction that you should go.

But if they don't take the time to do the research and aren't really up on current affairs and what's going on in the economy, then they're going to recommend diversification, because that protects them from their own lack of knowledge. And it's an easy sell: "Let's diversify, and some things will go up and some things will go down, and it'll work out for you." I happen to agree with Buffett. He probably could have described it a little nicer, but when you look at the facts, I think he's correct.

Just because you diversify with different risk-based assets doesn't mean that your money is going to be safe if we go through another market like the one we experienced in 2008, or if another September 11th should come along. No matter how diversified your portfolio is, it will lose value if it is tied to the market in such times.

The average amount of time that it takes to recover from a bear market is seven years. So, when you lose money in an investment, on average it takes you seven years to get back to even. The longest it has ever taken is about eighteen years. Our priority is to make sure our clients' money isn't all at risk. The result is it takes fewer years to get back to even when you have fewer losses in the first place.

The Buy-and-Hold Lie

"The recovery is on its way," your advisor or broker might say. "Wait it out. You'll be okay." That's pretty standard advice. Those who deal in risk-based assets have to project such optimism. Otherwise they would never tell you to put any money at risk. So they talk about how your portfolio will bounce back and you shouldn't fret over bumps in the road. They're not going to say to you, "Sorry, we took too much risk with your money and you lost it." Instead they put a spin on it and tell you that you haven't really lost anything unless you sell. "Unless you lock in your loss," they say, "you haven't really lost anything. It's just a paper loss."

That's ridiculous; If you had a statement that had $400,000 in assets and several months later it's $300,000, you lost money, whether you sell or not. That money is gone for now. But the broker is not going to tell you anything other than to just sit tight and ride it out. Obviously, he lost you a bunch of money and lacked the foresight to prevent it. The broker doesn't know what's going to happen next. He's just hoping that tomorrow will get better.

And if you don't get back to even and the broker is wrong again, it doesn't impact him. He's still collecting fees and commissions. He makes money whether you do or not. He isn't hoping you lose money. He wants your account to gain value, but it's no skin off his back if it doesn't.

The investor is the one who shoulders all of the risk. It's the retiree, or the potential retiree, who has everything to lose—not the advisor. When the advisor loses your money, he doesn't come running in the door with a bag of cash, saying, "Sorry, here you go, here's your money back." Instead, you'll hear: "These things happen, and you have to be okay with accepting risk. You need to buy and hold tight. This is just part of the deal when you have money in the market." In truth, having money in the market was the problem to begin with.

Where You Hear Good Advice

"Don't invest in things that are risky if you can't afford to lose that money." That's the advice we give. Such advice is usually going to come from an independent financial advisor that is not tied to a bank or a credit union or one of the large brokerage firms on Wall Street. It's usually going to be an independent advisory firm, prefer-ably somebody who specializes in working with retirees. That's where you really hear it most. Some independent advisors who work mainly with younger people might not have that safer money approach, but those who work with retirees have a fiduciary responsibility to the client. That's who you are going to hear it from.

CHAPTER 3

TODAY'S BETTER WAYS TO INVEST SAFELY

Most everyone wants a better rate of return than what a bank offers. That means they will take one of two options. There are two paths that you can go down with your money.

We've already seen what lies down the first one, the risk path. That's the one most advisors talk about: "To get a better rate, take some risk"—and then you will hear their line on diversifying. As we have seen, just because it was diversified didn't mean that it was safe. If you had money at risk, chances are you lost massively in 2008.

If you don't want to go down the risk path, the alternative when you're looking for a higher rate of return is to agree to a certain amount of time with your money. If you agree to put your money on deposit in an investment for a certain number of years before you're going to withdraw it, then you can get a better rate of return than what the bank will pay you.

Those alternatives include bonds with a certain number of years to maturity, as well as certain types of annuities. We frequently recommend fixed and indexed annuities because they typically allow you the opportunity to earn a better rate of return, but they can be just as safe as leaving the money on deposit in the bank.

Fixed and Indexed Annuities

One of the safest ways to invest your money today is a fixed annuity. Traditional fixed annuities, in one form or another, have been around since the age of the Roman Empire, used as way for governments to quickly finance wars and compensate soldiers. In the 1700s, many European countries used annuities in lieu of government bonds. And during the Great Depression, many astute Americans used the safety of fixed annuities to save themselves from financial ruin.

Fixed annuity guarantees are backed by the claims paying ability of the issuing insurance company, there are no fees and are tax deferred. But the thing to watch out for with a fixed annuity is that your interest rate is only going to be as good as the guarantee the company you are working with gives you. Sometimes those guarantees are very attractive, but sometimes they are not. Back in 1982, fixed annuities were paying a guaranteed 18 percent interest, with no fees, on a tax-deferred basis. It was a great time to have money in a fixed annuity. In recent years, the best fixed annuity rate you could likely find is around 4 percent. Rates are certainly not as high as they once were, but they may be a little higher than some of the other safe alternatives out there. Again, fixed annuities are very safe and have no fees—but you do have to watch out for low interest rates on those instruments.

Indexed annuities are relatively new in the United States, though they have existed over-seas for decades. They were offered in the U.S. for the first time in 1995, born out of the need for an even safer investment vehicle at a point in history when other types of annuities, as well as bonds, were not performing as expected and interest rates were spiraling downward. What's unique about indexed annuities is they allow you to participate in the upswings of the market, but never participate in the downswings. And along the way, both principal and growth are always protected because you're agreeing to a certain number of years before you withdraw everything.

Suppose you were to go to Las Vegas and put $100,000 on the table and spin the wheel. If you win, you might gain $10,000. If you lose, you get $50,000 back. So you have a $10,000 upside potential and a $50,000 downside potential. But imagine another game where you put your $100,000 up and if you win you might get $8,000, $9,000, or $10,000, and if you lose you get your $100,000 back. That's basically how the indexed annuity works.

With an indexed annuity, first you select an index (typically, it's the Standard & Poor's index, but there are other options). If the index you choose goes up in value for the chosen period, your account has the opportunity to participate in those gains. If that index goes down in value for the year, and your money is safe, secure and protected, and you won't lose a penny. When the market grows, your account grows with it; if the market drops, you don't lose anything. A nice feature of these accounts is that they not only protect your principal but also your growth. Let's say you start with $100,000 in an account and, over time, it grows to $150,000. Then, the economy and the stock market tank. No problem—you are protected at $150,000. You don't lose your principal or your growth. When the market begins to recover, you start right where you left off. You won't have a big hole to dig yourself out of.

Also, a good indexed annuity will not have annual fees or expenses. That, combined with the protection of your principal and growth potential make these products even more attractive. But some find this too good to be true, and I'm sure a few people reading this are thinking, "What's the catch?"

Of course you do not get all these benefits without a couple of strings that are attached. As good as indexed annuities are, two things can make them inappropriate for investors.

Indexed Annuities Aren't for Everyone

I mentioned that investment companies do not charge annual fees or expenses on indexed annuities, but do you think they do this out of the kindness of their corporate heart or because they are really nice people? No, of course not. They are in it to make money. But, rather than charging us fees and expenses, they make money on your money while it is on deposit with them, which is the same way a bank makes money on a CD. The bank does not charge you for a CD either, but they aren't doing it for free. They are making money on your CD money while it's on deposit with them.

This brings us to our first string that's attached, something called *time horizon*. How long can you wait before you need access to 100 percent of your money? The marketplace's sweet spot is somewhere between four and ten years. If you have at least four years before you will be taking all the money out of the account, then the indexed annuity might be appropriate. During this initial four-year period, it is not as if you put your money in jail where you can't get to it. You are able to take some of money out of the account each year if you need or want to, but you don't have to. But you can't take everything out, all at once, for at least four years (unless you have a major medical emergency or must go into a nursing home). Otherwise, you can only take part of the money. At four years, you can move it somewhere else, or you can leave it there. What you do with it at that point is completely up to you.

I meet with individuals frequently who say, "Matt, I have this account that I want to roll over, and I want to use an indexed annuity, but in 18 months I'll be buying a vacation home"—or a boat, or whatever. An indexed annuity will not work for that. You need at least four years before you can take it out. So the first string attached is *time horizon*.

The second string that's attached is called *maximum gain*. Since you never participate in market downturns with an indexed annuity, companies set a maximum that you can earn during the "good" years. Depending on the company and the strategy, your maximum gain may be between 8 and 25 percent for the year. Twenty-five percent is about the highest you could ever see it calculated. It is possible that the market could grow more than the maximum gain your account allows. On the flip side, you have none of the downside risk, because on years when the market loses 10, 20, or 30 percent, you might not make any money, but you are not going to lose any, either. The worst that can happen is you earn zero percent interest for the year. Those are years when we say, "Zero is a hero." What you are doing is giving up some of the upside potential in the stock market to have none of the downside risk.

INDEXED ANNUITY VS. STOCK MARKET

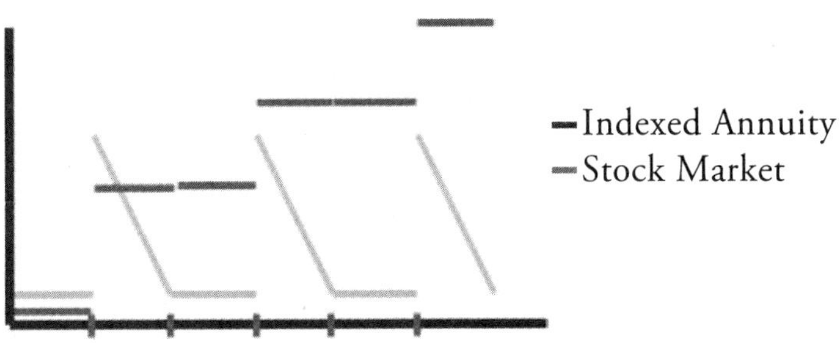

Indexed annuities are one of the best-kept secrets in the financial services industry, but, depending on your investment goals, you do need to be mindful of their time horizon and maximum gain. You give up some liquidity and potentially some of the upside in the market. But no investor is upset when the market is falling and he has exactly the same amount of money in his account as when the downturn began.

Beware the Variable Annuity

A word of warning about a third type of tax-deferred annuity account is the *variable annuity,* which does put your money at risk. In the media, you'll hear talking heads proclaiming that you should not put your money in annuities. Typically, they're talking about variable annuities, and they're telling you this because the annual fees and expenses associated with them can be outrageous. Typical variable annuities have annual fees between 2 and 6 percent. I have seen them as high as 8 percent, but on average they're around 4 percent.

Let's say you have $100,000 in a variable annuity with a 4 percent annual fee, which means you pay $4,000 per year for the management of that account. Over a ten-year period, you could pay as much as $40,000 in fees on that $100,000 account. In my opinion, this is one of the biggest rip-offs in the financial services industry. If you don't already have a variable annuity, do not get one. Most people who come to me with variable annuities are shocked when they realize the fees they are paying.

Here is a scenario that plays out in my office almost every week. Some individuals own variable annuities and don't even know it. Others may know it fully well. They'll tell me, "I called my advisor. I have a low-cost variable annuity, and all I'm paying is 1.4 percent." If someone is told anything less than 2 percent, I will request that we double check and verify that number. I have a speaker phone in my conference room and, with the client's permission, I can call the 1-800 number on the statement or contract. I can phone directly into the home office of the variable annuity and validate the fees.

This usually takes no more than five minutes. Some investors will be led to believe they're paying something around 1 to 2 percent; but after five minutes on the phone, I'll find out they are really paying between 2 and 6 percent.

I have been in this profession for many years, and I have seen this many times. The fees are almost never as low as the advisors say they are. Some advisors do not understand all of the fees. Typical variable annuities will have four or five types of annual fees charged to the account each year. They have mortality and expense fees, management fees, administrative fees, trading costs, annual fees and rider charges. When you put them all together, they'll add up to an average of 4 percent. Most advisors will know about one or two of the fees, but they should know about *all* of them—and so should you.

In addition to its fees, a variable annuity leaves you 100 percent exposed to the volatility of the stock market. You can fully participate in the gains of the market when it is doing well, but when it is performing poorly, you will also fully participate in its losses. This is not what safe money is about.

RULE TWO

Get a Reasonable Return

CHAPTER 4

FEES THAT PICK YOUR POCKET

You cannot claim that you are truly investing safely if you don't have a reasonable return. After all, you need to earn enough on your investments to offset inflation and to provide sufficient income so that you can deal with the emergencies and contingencies that arise in everyone's life. If your finances don't offer that kind of protection, they are hardly serving you well.

One way to boost your investment power is to keep fees to a minimum. A lot of times, when people consider the fees they are paying, they assume they amount to perhaps 1 or 2 percent per year—which doesn't really sound like a lot. But let's take a look at one of today's most common investments, the mutual fund, and see what's really happening.

WHY SO MANY MUTUAL FUNDS?

Mutual funds were established because investors were finding it difficult to choose the right equities out of the multitude available. In a mutual fund, they could buy into a collection of stocks or bonds and depend upon a fund manager to take care of the investment details. This was supposed to simplify the situation.

The mutual fund industry has been spending about ten billion dollars a year on marketing, and today in this country we have more mutual funds to choose from than individual stocks. One must wonder why. Why are there so many mutual funds? It probably has something to do with the generous fees and commissions that they pay to the advisors that sell them and the firms those advisors work for.

Every mutual fund today has what's called a management fee, and it's usually 1 or 2 percent annually, but it can be a lot higher. It's rarely less than 1 percent. The national average is a 1.5 percent management fee. Let's say you have $100,000 in a mutual fund, and you pay 1.5 percent. That means that you'll lose $1,500 per year. To some people, that sounds like a lot of money. Others might say that's not so bad, because you do have to pay something for the services. The problem that I have with these types of fees is the fact that you have to pay them every year. Whether the mutual fund goes up or goes down in value, you're going to pay the fee year after year—and in a decade, that 1.5 percent means you will lose about $15,000 on a $100,000 account.

But that's just one of the fees. Mutual funds also have what's called a turnover cost, or a trading cost. The mutual fund manager is buying and selling securities, and every time he does, there's a cost for that. It's not free. Typically, each of those transactions cost about 1 percent. When you consider a mutual fund, you want to know what its management fee is, but you also want to know how much turnover that fund has. The higher the turnover, the higher the trading costs. If a mutual fund has a 50 percent turnover rate, that means that half the assets over the last twelve months were sold and new ones were bought. You multiply that 50 percent turnover by the 1 percent trading cost, and you get an additional half a percent in fees. Add that to the management fee, you're now up to 2 percent for your fees. But some mutual funds have turnovers of 200 percent or even 500 percent. Sometimes they conduct a massive amount of frequent trading. Every time they do, that costs you money. If you have 400 percent turnover in your mutual fund and a 1.5 percent management fee, that means you're paying 5.5 percent a year in fees. Again, over a ten-year period, that's an enormous amount of money that you lose.

Those are two fees that basically every mutual fund has. Then in addition to those fees, I'll sometimes see that people are paying account fees, or annual fees. That's usually some nominal amount, maybe fifty to one-hundred dollars a year just to have the account. A lot of times people see that fee on the statement, and they think that's all that they're paying, but they're certainly paying much more.

Yet another type of fee they may be paying is called an advisory fee, or a wrap fee. That's a fee that the advisor is charging. Sometimes it's called a money management fee. Generally it's 1 to 2 percent per year, on top of all the other fees that we've just mentioned.

When you add up all the fees, investors often are paying 3 to 6 percent per year, every year, and most of the time they have no idea they're paying that much. "My advisor said all I'm paying him is 1 percent," I often hear. And that might be true. But the mutual fund fees still apply. Your advisor doesn't get any of those fees, but you're still paying them. The financial institutions make out well—and I'm sure you get the picture on why there are so many mutual funds.

Strategic Wealth Report

In our office, we offer what we call a Strategic Wealth Report, where people can bring in their statements and we can research and figure out exactly what they're paying in fees. We show the percentage and dollar amounts of what they're paying and how much would be lost to fees over ten years.

Sometimes people protest that there's no way the companies could be charging these fees without their knowing it—"They would tell me about them," clients sometimes tell me. That's true. They have to let you know how much they're charging in fees, but they do so through the prospectus that they send you in the mail. The fees are disclosed in those thick documents. Few people take the time to read a prospectus. It's not exactly scintillating reading. But they've told you. They've fulfilled their legal obligation to notify you.

But they don't make it easy for you. Even if you were to read that prospectus, you would find it difficult to locate the fees. That's why they are called hidden fees. Most do not appear on your statements. You never get a bill or invoice; they deduct the fees automatically from your account. If you were to read the prospectus you might find one of the fees on page 12, another one on page 28, and then another maybe on page 57. You have to read the entire prospectus and understand what it is that it is saying and how it impacts you and your money. You have to track down the fees, figure out the percentages, and add them up. Most people do not have the time or the desire to do this on their own, which is why we created the Strategic Wealth Report; we can do it for you.

All of the fees can add up. If your fees total 3 percent, that means your fund might only grow by 7 percent if the stock market rose 10 percent. If the market fell 10 percent, your loss could be 13 percent because of the fees. They drag down your account over time because they act like an anchor, and they can have an enormous impact on how much money you have for your retirement.

You Might be Better Off Investing in an Index Fund

I am not against mutual funds completely. I have a securities license. I have clients who have owned mutual funds, and I, too, have owned mutual funds in the past. Mutual funds have a time and place. The problem is that a lot of advisors have convinced the public that mutual funds are the only options out there, and now far too many people have way too much of their assets tied up in them as a result. Why, you ask, is that a problem?

Studies show that when you invest money in a mutual fund, it will perform worse, about 80 percent of the time, than the benchmark or index that the fund manager is trying to beat. The performance of every mutual fund is gauged against a certain outside benchmark (typically the Standard & Poor's financial index, but there are others), and that index usually does better.

Think about that. You could invest in the index for little or no cost, while mutual fund investments are never free. A close review of mutual funds can reveal annual fees, account fees, management fees, trading costs, wrap fees, inactivity fees, and low balance fees. It seems as though they have a fee and expense for everything they can think of. Those fees, as we have seen, are costing you dearly, and you usually are not getting good performance in return.

Mutual fund reports tell us that it could cost as much as 5 percent, upfront, to invest money in the fund. I often meet people who tell me their mutual fund is free every year because they already paid all their fees as an "upfront load." But that's not the whole story. If you pay an upfront load or commission when you put your money into a mutual fund, you are still paying the ongoing management fee and trading costs. You end up paying significant costs for the privilege of doing worse than the index—and again, the index may be free, or nearly so. The mutual fund industry doesn't want that type of information out there.

Double Dipping

One way to cut back on the high fees and expenses is to work with advisors who don't do what I call "double dip accounts"—in other words, you pay the advisor a wrap fee or advisory fee, and the advisor turns around and invests the money in mutual funds.

You're hiring them to be a money manager, and all they do is hire other money managers. You're just adding another layer of fees. If you're going to pay an advisor a fee to manage your money, they shouldn't bring additional fees to your portfolio. They should be able to buy individual stocks or bonds, ETF's, preferred stocks, annuities and other securities.

If you're going to have money in a mutual fund, there's no way to avoid the fees. You can do the research and we can help you find one with lower costs, if you want, but always remember: Those fees are lining the pockets of fund managers and brokers, to the detriment of your retirement livelihood. It would be naïve to think that the advice you are getting is free. It comes at great cost, and it isn't made apparent to you.

For many years, investors were led to believe that mutual funds were the only option. Advisors acted as though they were the only place to invest money, and that's just not the case. But in recent years the introduction of new products has helped to stem the flow of money into mutual funds dramatically. Investors have become more educated and have realized there are other alternatives out there. Some have gotten a look behind the curtain and don't necessarily like what they've seen. Mutual funds are still, by far, where most people have their retirement assets, and that's not going to change anytime soon. But slowly and surely, investors are looking to alternatives.

CHAPTER 5

KEEPING TAXES UNDER CONTROL

I spend countless hours educating people about the impact that their tax strategy—if they have one—will have on their wealth. I am no longer shocked, but often I'm still amazed, that so little attention is given to how assets will be taxed, whether during investment or distribution. I believe that how an investment will be treated from a tax perspective is of utmost importance.

Virtually everyone I talk to feels as if he or she is paying too much in taxes. Even people in the lowest tax bracket feel that whatever they are paying is unfair and somebody else should pay more. And yet, if you look at the history of taxation in the United States, you will see that today we are in one of the lowest tax environments ever.

U.S. citizens started paying federal income taxes in 1913—the country got along a long time without them. At the time, Congress promised us that the lowest bracket for federal income taxes would be 1 percent and that the top federal bracket would never be greater than 5 percent.

That promise was broken early and often. In recent years the top federal tax bracket has been near 40% percent. However, that's still one of the lowest the country has seen.

If you look all the way back to 1913, the top federal bracket has averaged around 50 percent. The highest it has ever been was 94 percent, back in the 1940s for two years. During the 1940s and 50s, we spent a decade where the top federal bracket was at 90 percent or above.

One wonders, in those years when the tax bracket was so high, what incentive millionaires had to try build their enterprises. In the days when President Reagan was an actor, if he made any more movies than one per year, his income on the additional movies was taxed at 90 percent. It just wasn't the American way, he felt, to have citizens working for a dime on the dollar—why would he make more than one movie a year? That's really what drove him into politics. When he came into office, he cut taxes in half, for the most part. He cut the brackets in half to get them down to a more reasonable level.

No Way To Go But Up

So historically speaking, today's top tax bracket isn't all that high. Which raises this question: What do you think is going to happen moving forward?

Taxes really can't go any lower. With the debts and the deficits, at some point taxes will be going up, no matter who wins the next election or who controls Congress. They're not just going to go up for the rich, they're going to go up for everyone. The country can't keep spending at these levels and racking up such debts and deficits without taking steps to get more revenue. Congress hardly has a reputation for cutting costs. What it always seems to do is look for more revenue. With taxes at historical lows, they can only go one way. They're not going any lower. Nobody has a crystal ball, but that much seems certain.

The tax code is written to give people certain tax breaks even within the top bracket. There are ways to shield money for those who avail themselves of them. It is far from unpatriotic to take advantage of provisions of the tax code. The government isn't going to go out of its way to tell you about those breaks, but they are legitimate. Nobody should pay any more in tax than the legal requirement.

Often, wealthy people will invest in assets that pay dividends—and the top federal tax rate on dividends is currently 15 percent. That dividend rate has existed in this country for many, many years. There has been recent populist political talk that the dividend rate gives an unfair advantage to the wealthy and should be raised to 45 percent. Those who espouse that view tend to leave out the fact that those dividends often come at great risk to the investor, who is injecting a lot of money into the markets and economy.

There have been other proposals to do away with the mortgage interest rate deduction and the deduction for charitable contributions. Some want to increase taxes on businesses. They've proposed taking away tax deductions for private companies if they own a private plane. Such talk is popular among politicians, particularly during an election year. It strikes a chord with many people who feel taking away such tax breaks would curb greed and excess. But they don't think about how such policies affect the economy. They can hurt industries and cost people their jobs. It takes a lot of people to build a corporate plane, for example. You have to employ a lot of people to construct, repair and maintain it, and hire pilots to fly it.

Are they really going to take away the corporate tax deduction for planes? Probably not. Are they going to do away with your deductions for charitable contributions? Probably not. That would be an awful scenario for many good causes. Are they going to do away with the mortgage deduction for the interest on your house? Probably not. What do we think would happen to housing prices if they were to do that? They'd go even lower. That's not going to help anybody or anything.

What happens instead is that they take the 15 percent tax bracket and turn it into a 25 percent tax bracket. They take the 35 percent tax bracket and increase it to a 50 percent tax bracket. They always come back and they go after the federal tax brackets and the dividend tax bracket. All those other proposals just amount to attempts to get votes and get people excited and rallying behind them, but in reality those ideas are never pursued. The politicians do the easy thing, which is simply to make you pay.

You're better off trying to get your money into tax deferred or tax free accounts now, before the rates go higher and we lose some of the loopholes that are available today. You want to get the money in there now, so those dollars can grow tax deferred. If tax rates return to 40 or 60 percent—hopefully, they will never go back to 90 percent—you will have money in tax free accounts that you can access. It won't really matter what the tax rate is at that time.

Social Security and Taxes

Over the years, the Social Security income threshold has gone up—meaning the amount of money that a retiree can earn before his or her benefit is subjected to taxation. When Social Security was started, back in the 1930s, there was no threshold.

Social Security originally was a voluntary program. You did not have to participate. Only later did it become mandatory. The tax rate on workers originally was very low—1 or 2 percent was all the government was going to charge us, and now we are up to 6.2 percent plus the tax that you pay for Medicare. Over the years, the tax rate has slowly been increasing.

The government has quite a problem. When Social Security was started, you had to be sixty-five to qualify for it. Life expectancy then was sixty-six. Few people were expected to receive the benefit for very long. Today, you can take the benefit as early as sixty-two. You can take it earlier than that if you're disabled or for other specified reasons. Meanwhile, life expectancy is getting longer and longer. A lot of my clients are planning on living into their eighties, at least. Some of them are in their nineties. They're spending many years on Social Security.

Social Security in reality is just a massive Ponzi scheme. People who are working and paying money into it must support the people who are retired and taking money out. There is no real trust fund. It's funded by taxes and revenue coming into the overall system. To keep it afloat, the government has increased the tax rates, and it will have to do much more to keep the system solvent in the years to come. Taxes will have to rise even more. There have been discussions about taking the cap off the Social Security tax so that you would pay it on all of your income.

In the future it is likely that retirees will be subjected to means testing before receiving a Social Security benefit. If you have been successful and you have accumulated money—in other words, if you have the means—then you wouldn't get anything out of the Social Security trust fund. Those who work hard to make and save a lot of money are going to have to pay more into the system, and then when they retire they probably aren't going to get anything out of it.

You can debate the merits of Social Security, but the bottom line is that we've decided as a nation that we're going to have it, so we're going to keep it. The only way to fix it at this point is to dramatically alter it from the state that it's in now. That's going to include increasing tax rates, delaying when you can take the benefit, and minimizing the number of people who are eligible to draw from it.

Meanwhile, a "tax free" investment such as municipal bonds isn't necessarily without tax for a retiree collecting Social Security. The investment remains free of federal tax, but the income from that investment counts toward that threshold that we have discussed—the amount you're allowed to earn before your Social Security benefit is taxed.

Many people also are concerned that the government will weaken Roth IRAs. Roth IRAs right now grow tax free, and you take the money out tax free. However, many people are concerned that Congress will change that and find a way to make it taxable for some. If you have a large net worth or a large income, the politicians may try to subject you to means testing on that as well.

It's important to keep up to date on changes in the law and tax policy, so that if it looks as if any of these tax laws are going to change, you can take appropriate action and choose options to protect your money.

TAX-FREE, TAX-DEFERRED, AND TAXABLE INVESTING

When discussing taxes in this country, we have three ways that we can grow our money. We have taxable accounts, tax-deferred accounts, and tax-free accounts. Let's look at some examples on how each method will affect you.

First, we will look at growing our money tax-free, as in a Roth IRA/401k or an overfunded life insurance contract. Let's say we invest a dollar and, every year, that dollar doubles in value without any tax. And let's say we do this for twenty consecutive years. What will the dollar grow to? In other words, one dollar grows to two, then four, then eight, then sixteen, and we do this for twenty years. How much money will you have? When I ask that question, the most typical response is, "A lot!" And that is correct. You would have just over $1,000,000 if you did not have to pay any tax on the gains.

But let's say we decide to grow our money in a taxable account. This could be a taxable mutual fund or CDs. Again, we double our dollar every year for twenty years, but this time, along the way, we have to pay taxes out of the account at 28 percent each year. How much will we have at the end of the twenty years? Most people would guess $720,000. Others guess $500,000. But neither number is close, because you would be left with only about $57,000 after tax.

What has happened is that taxes have robbed us of compound interest. Albert Einstein was quoted as saying that compound interest is the eighth wonder of the world—and it is, until the IRS gets ahold of it.

There is a third way that you can grow your money, and that is tax-deferred. We can't always grow money tax-free, but we can almost always grow money tax-deferred. Let's look at our example again. If you have a dollar and it doubles every year for twenty years in a tax-deferred account, at the end of the twenty years you will have just over $1,000,000 because you never had to pay any taxes. Of course, you will have to pay taxes on that money when you take it out, right? Let's assume you took all of the money out in one year (most investors wouldn't do this, but bear with me). If you took all of the money out in the same year, you would most likely be left with around $600,000 after tax. That is not as good as the $1,000,000 you would have in the tax-free account, but it is at least ten times better than what you would have in the taxable account.

Growing Wealth Without Taxes

Where do you keep your money? The conclusion should be clear: It's best to grow your wealth in tax free accounts if you can. If not, the second best option is to defer the tax. Only emergency funds should be left in taxable accounts; otherwise, the cost is too great.

The Roth IRA is a prime example of a tax free investment, but you need to qualify to open one. There are income limitations—you can't open an account if you make too much money or if you don't have any earned income. If you qualify, you do not get a tax deduction for your contributions, but any growth will be tax free. If you withdraw funds in the future, you will owe no tax.

Municipal bonds also provide you with interest that is tax free, though the rate generally isn't all that high. However, typically the rate will be better than a CD—and CDs require you to pay tax on the interest earned.

Overfunded life insurance contracts, which could be an appropriate investment for some people, are a third example of tax free investments. Most people don't realize this, but permanent life insurance in this country today includes the advantage of tax free growth of assets. If you have a really bad permanent life insurance plan, you will be facing a variety of costs, and the interest you get might only be 1 or 2 percent. That has given life insurance a reputation as a bad investment, but high-quality companies keep fees low and offer what is called an overfunded plan. That means you put more money than required into it. That increases the cash you have in the plan, which raises the dividend. You might be able to realize a dividend of 6, 7, or 8 percent on a permanent insurance plan—and you won't need to pay tax on that growth.

Don't Pay Tax on Reinvested Money

I meet people regularly who keep their retirement funds in CDs and other taxable accounts. They have that money earmarked for retirement. Take note of this fundamental of sound money management: You don't want to pay taxes on income that you are not currently using for living expenses. If you have a CD, when it matures it's going to pay some interest. That interest is taxable income. If you roll that money back into a new CD, you are not using that income for living expenses. But you are paying tax on it nonetheless. Uncle Sam will take his cut, and that will significantly slow the growth of your investment.

Instead, you need to grow your money in a tax efficient manner, using investment vehicles that will not create a taxable event—and that is what you have created when you roll a maturing CD into a new one. You earned interest, and those earnings must be reported on your tax return the following year.

Triple Taxation on Mutual Funds

When you hold a mutual fund in a regular taxable account, you face the prospect of what is called triple taxation. A lot of investors and advisors are unaware of what is happening: There are three different taxes you have to pay.

The first is a short-term capital gains tax. Every time the fund manager sells a stock or bond without having held it for at least twelve months, that creates a short term capital gain. Let's say your mutual fund grows by 10 percent in value for the year. Let's say that 100 percent of the fund was turned over, which is not unusual at all. In that case, all of that 10 percent gain is going to be taxed, and it's taxed at short term capital gain rates, which is whatever federal and state and local income tax bracket that you are in. If you're in the 20, 30, or 40 percent bracket, that's how much you lose in tax. Say you're in a 30 percent tax bracket. If your mutual fund went up by 10 percent but you had to pay 30 percent in tax, the net return to you really was only 7 percent. You had to give the rest of it to the IRS.

The second tax is a long-term capital gains tax. This one's pretty simple. You buy the mutual fund at $20 a share, and over time it goes up in value and you sell it at some point in the future for thirty dollars per share. You're going to have to pay long-term capital gains taxes on that growth. You made $10 per share. For most people, that would be taxed at 15 percent.

The third tax—and this is the one that a lot of people aren't aware of—is the dividend tax. Most mutual funds in this country today will declare some sort of a dividend. They do so because the stocks or the bonds in the fund are likewise creating dividends and interest. What most people do is reinvest the dividend to buy more shares of the mutual fund. I'm not arguing whether that's a bad strategy, but just because you took that dividend to buy more shares does not mean that you don't owe any tax on the income that was created from that mutual fund.

You still have to pay tax, whether you take the dividend out or you use it to buy more shares in the mutual fund. This particular dividend, the way that it's structured, is taxed at ordinary income tax rates. Again, if you're in a 20, 30, or 40 percent bracket, that's how much you lose in tax, even though you reinvested the money. This tax is why people got a tax bill at the end of 2008 after mutual fund values had fallen precipitously. They had to pay tax on the dividends that were declared.Holding mutual funds in taxable accounts over a long period of time is one of the worst things people can do. Again, we see it all the time. But if you have a mutual fund, you want it at least to be in a tax deferred account, if not a tax free one. I cannot emphasize that enough.

MUTUAL FUNDS
=
TRIPLE TAXATION

A big reason that most people don't focus on taxes as much as they should is that their advisors never really bring the matter up. Investors too often think only of their rate of return and do not consider the long-term impact that taxes can have. Tax strategy can spell the difference between success or failure once you get into retirement. When your money goes into the government's coffers, it stops working to grow your portfolio. Opportunity is lost, at great cost.

Chapter 6

Managed Money Philosophy

Let's talk about proper asset management. Many people, including some advisors, believe that investing money into a diversified portfolio, typically, a mixture of stocks, bonds, mutual funds, and exchange traded funds, is proper asset management. But it isn't.

One myth in investing is that it's all about diversification. While it's true that you don't want to have all of your eggs in one basket, real diversification is the goal and that means utilizing different asset categories. Some individuals will buy twenty different stocks or twenty different mutual funds and think that they're diversified. That isn't the case at all if all those stocks and mutual funds are invested in the same market or the same economy. You need to have diversification of economies *and* diversification of asset categories. Within your portfolio, it may be appropriate for you to have some portion of your money in stocks, bonds, real estate, commodities, precious metals, treasuries or any number of other asset categories—or none of them.

Whether you talk with a professional or determine your objectives on your own, proper asset management begins with understanding exactly what you're trying to accomplish both in the short term and long term. Investments are then selected based upon what aligns with your goals and future objectives and this is typically referred to as asset allocation. More specifically this means implementing a strategy that balances risk with reward by adjusting the amount invested in different asset classes to align with a client's goals, risk tolerance and time horizon.

Many times, what happens in this industry is that advisors know what they're going to recommend before the client walks into their office or even shares their desired outcome. This is because they have some one-size-fits-all product to sell based on a sales quota or marketing support deal with one of their vendors. What you should be looking for in an advisor is someone that will take you through a discovery process, as opposed to selling or recommending a product to you.

You do not want to work with someone that appears to understand proper asset allocation on the front end, and then does what we refer to as the "set it and forget it" approach. These are the advisors that, when the market gets volatile, and you inquire about what you should do to prevent losing money during a stock market correction, will say things to like, "Don't worry about it because you're in it for the long run. If you lose money in the market, it'll bounce back. It always does. You don't need that money right now anyway. You know, it's just a paper loss, you don't lose anything unless you sell."

Unfortunately, most of the industry is taught simply to asset gather, creating what they refer to as a diversified portfolio. And then ... they set it and forget it. They sit back, collect their fees annually, and maybe, they'll rebalance and adjust things occasionally. For the most part, they're done. They won't do any additional work or be proactive, even if the market is down sharply.

Again, you don't want to work with someone that takes a one-size-fits-all approach. Your desire should be to work with someone that understands true diversification. Every individual, when investing money in the stock market, will have varying degrees of risk tolerance and will need different potential rates of return. Someone looking for income shouldn't have the same type of investments used when someone's looking for growth or just safety. There are different types of approaches for different outcomes and you want to work with a firm that recognizes this. Every investment manager should have different portfolios representing different risk and reward scenarios that they can use individually or in combination to match the individual client's needs.

If you're hiring an advisor to help you with your retirement assets, you should be working with someone that will keep you informed. Regular communication with your advisor is crucial. Even if things are steady and stable within the stock markets, you should still be informed and understand exactly what's happening with your money. Changes should also be made to your portfolio anytime you have a major life event, such as getting married, having a child, or unfortunately, going through a divorce, or death of a loved one. And of course, the big one everyone should be concerned about is retirement. All along the way, the portfolio manager should be paying attention, and then adjusting as needed or required.

As mentioned in a previous chapter, you also want to be mindful of the fees you're being charged. It's always best to avoid fees altogether if possible, but when it's not you want to make sure that what you're being charged is reasonable. What is reasonable? I would argue in today's environment that anything below 2 percent is reasonable depending on the level of service you're being provided and the amount of assets you invest. Additionally, fees should be disclosed and documented up front so that you know exactly what you're paying.

The team at Strategic Wealth Designers specializes in asset management and our portfolios provide comprehensive asset allocation. We diversify risks and target the rate of return the client is seeking. Customization to each individual investor's needs is important, so our suite of portfolios cover a range of return and asset categories. Although no one has a crystal ball, a good advisor's job, with a relative amount of predictability, is to anticipate what's going to happen in the stock market and adjust their portfolios. We pay close attention to what's happening in the economy and markets and make adjustments accordingly. And while we don't make changes to our portfolios every day, we are monitoring them daily. Even when the economy is running smoothly, adjustments to portfolios should still be made. We aim to rebalance things no more than two or three times per year but will adjust more often if we see some volatility; possibly increasing our cash position to act as a hedge against a fall in stock market.

Our method is to use technical analysis to remove all of the emotions from investing, and part of that process is utilizing software. The program we use runs a risk analysis every evening that the stock market is open and essentially stress tests our portfolios so we can take action if there's something we need to pay a little closer attention to. The software we utilize has over one-hundred years' worth of historical data, and while no two events are identical, almost anything that could possibly happen in the stock market will be similar to something that has happened in the past- and we can test for it. Additionally, we have an investment council that meets at least quarterly and sometimes more often than that if there is volatility that would warrant making structural adjustments.

One of the things most investors don't realize is that the stock market tries to anticipate and "price in" what it believes is going to happen. So if we wait to make adjustments until an actual event has already occurred, at that point it's too late and it's already been priced into the market. A practical example of this is when the Federal Reserve holds their regular meeting and is expected to either increase or decrease interest rates. In anticipation of this, the market will typically react four to six weeks (sometimes as much as two to three months) in advance. And when the Fed surprises or disappoints us by not acting in accordance with what the consensus was, that's when you'll see dramatic moves either up or down in the stock market. Our software can test for these kinds of events to make sure we're prepared no matter what the economy throws our way. All of this helps us to stay informed on what's happening in the markets, but more importantly to keep our portfolios in line with what our clients' objectives are.

Our goal in communicating with our clients is to reach them no less than once per month with updates on the economy and stock market. We accomplish this through podcasts, newsletters, social media updates, emails with informative videos as well as our educational events like Wine & Wisdom. This keeps us connected and all contributes to keeping our clients abreast of what we're seeing in the economy and stock market. Our clients really enjoy these many types of interactions. And they deserve that—you deserve that.

Regarding fees, we look at our clients' portfolios holistically and target an aggregate fee structure of approximately 1 percent or less. We can accomplish that by mixing in products that have no fees along with our managed portfolios that do carry fees. However, any fees charged are fully disclosed and documented up front in the Investment Advisory Contract. There's no hidden fees or expenses that clients are unaware of and individuals can make an informed decision whether they want to move forward. If they do end up becoming managed portfolio clients, fees are clearly detailed on their monthly statements and when we do our full annual reviews, this data is examined and discussed. Unlike many institutions, our fee structure is completely transparent, and clients know exactly what their costs are and how fees are affecting their portfolio.

RULE THREE

Keep It Simple

CHAPTER 7

OUR GRANDPARENTS' SECRET

Most people associate grandparents with a simpler time. Typically, you went to work for one company and you put in your thirty or forty years and then you retired with Social Security and a pension. And you had two kids and a three or four-bedroom house with a white picket fence. That was the American dream.

In today's global and Internet economy with the multitude of marketing messages aimed at us daily, life can feel complex and confusing. It seems far from the principles of our forebears: to live within your means, to contribute to charity or your place of worship, to set aside money for a rainy day—and retirement. Live right, don't overspend, and things will work out. We've gotten away from that.

We have our mortgages and our credit cards, and we buy things that wc cannot afford and that we don't need. Once, you would rarely see a BMW or Porsche. They seemed rare. Not anymore. And it's not necessarily because people make a lot more money than they did a generation or two ago. We've gotten caught up in this mentality of trying to keep up with the Joneses. Everybody wants satisfaction now, and they're not willing to wait or pay their dues to enjoy it a little later in life.

It's unlikely people with that attitude will put much money aside for retirement. We should get back to some basics. It doesn't need to be overly confusing and complex if you just follow some simple guidelines. Trying to live a life you can't afford does not lead to success.

People have told me that they're worried that they will be worse off than their grandparents, or not as well prepared for retirement. They don't know exactly what their grandparents' retirement plans were, but they do know that they lived fairly comfortably in their retirement. I tell my clients that I have a pretty good idea of how their grandparents probably accomplished it. They did it by not taking any risk, by putting their money in safe investments, and by living frugally—so that they had more money to put into those investments.

Therefore they had more money for retirement. People lose that opportunity today. Not only are they manic about keeping up with the Joneses, but they feel they deserve a Caribbean vacation, or they really need a seventy-two inch Next Gen TV in the family room. And they're going to go get it whether they can really afford it or not. They buy things on credit that they really don't have any business purchasing. And the cost of the opportunity they are losing is staggering.

Success Doesn't Come by Default

I meet some people, especially younger ones, who have an entitlement attitude. They have a four-year degree so they think they deserve a company car, a corner office, eight weeks of vacation, and much more.

It's as if we've lost the fundamental value that,"it's up to me." You have to go out there and really work for it. Nobody's going to hand it to you. You deserve an opportunity to be successful, but you don't deserve to be successful by default.

It comes down to being willing to do what it takes. Successful people make a habit of doing things that unsuccessful people aren't willing to do. People who are financially successful tend not to over spend and buy things they can't really afford. They may wait to accumulate the cash first before they make the purchase. They don't buy fancy cars until they have put aside all they can for their retirement.

> SUCCESSFUL PEOPLE MAKE A HABIT OF DOING THINGS THAT UNSUCCESSFUL PEOPLE AREN'T WILLING TO DO.

I paid my own way to go to college. I was the youngest of three boys. My parents could definitely have afforded to send me to college, but my dad was the youngest of eleven and he grew up in a time when you had to work for what you wanted. So all three of us heard this from our parents: "We don't pay for college."

When I first started my career, I was only eighteen years old and in college. With my earnings based completely on commissions, I worked in downtown Louisville during college to make money for my tuition. I didn't feel that I could afford to use a parking garage. I discovered that there was a parking lot where you could park for free if you got in before 7 a.m., but once the guard arrived you had to pay the fee. That parking lot was about four blocks from the office, so I would get down there before 7 a.m. and then walk four blocks in pouring rain, freezing cold, burning heat. It didn't matter. That's where I had to park. Each day I walked back and forth, twenty minutes or more each way. That's what I did for the first couple of years because I wanted to reinvest my earnings into my business. I didn't want to spend it on parking.

As I got busier I hired my very first assistant. Others told me I couldn't expect him to pay for parking. "You will need to give him a parking pass for the garage across the street," they said. So I did that. Meanwhile, I was still walking those four blocks—until eventually I got to the point where I realized that I was wasting nearly an hour a day walking back and forth from that parking lot. It made sense for me to get my own pass for the garage across the street, right next to the building. I could be more productive.

When I finally got my first parking pass, I reserved the best, most expensive spot I could get. It was right up front, next to the gate. When I finally felt I had become successful enough to afford it, I rewarded myself, because I had worked really hard to get that parking pass. Others in the office often would comment, "Hey, I saw your car. You got a great parking spot. How in the world did you get so lucky?" I'd have to laugh. Luck had nothing to do with it.

The Power of Sacrifice

By getting that parking space, I was able to use my time more productively, on more lucrative pursuits. But before I could get to that point, I had to be willing to do things that others just weren't willing to do. And that's what I've done my entire life. I've sacrificed and waited.

My brothers and I weren't surprised by my parents' philosophy about paying for college. Both my parents came from a very humble background. They never lived on the street, and they were never starving, but there wasn't much money. My dad's father was a shoe repairman. There were thirteen people in one house, his mom and dad and eleven kids. They had one bathroom. My dad had to sleep in a chair as a child. When my mother met him, he had three shirts and two of them were hand-me-downs from his older brothers.

My mother was one of four children, and her parents got a divorce back when you didn't get divorced. My grandmother raised the kids, and she worked many years as a butcher in a meat packing factory. You can see how family values were passed down to my brothers and me: At a very young age we were all taught that if you really want something, you have to go out there and work for it.

We all knew that our parents would give us all the love and support we needed until we were eighteen, and that when we turned eighteen we were adults. The deal that they gave us was that we could live at home for free as long as we were in college full time. Otherwise we had to pay rent and we had to buy our own food and do all the things that you have to do when you're an adult. There was nothing secret about what would be expected of us.

I did find out one thing that irritated me a bit when I was a sophomore in college, struggling financially. I was living at home to save money, but I was otherwise on my own and had to pay all my own expenses. My father, when he was a boy, had worked to pay part of his tuition to go to a private high school. He was the only one of the eleven siblings to receive a college degree, but at the time they had thought he was crazy to pay to go to the high school. While I was in college, I learned that my father had funded a scholarship for an underprivileged child to go to his high school for free. The tuition for that high school cost more than the tuition for the university that I was attending.

"Wait a minute," I thought, "I'm struggling here, paying my own way, barely able to afford shoes—and my father is paying the way for a complete stranger?" What was that all about? It bothered me.

But then I started thinking about a lot of my friends whose parents paid for them to go to college. Some of them didn't show up for class and got poor grades. Some failed and had to leave college. My attitude was that if I was paying for it, I was going to show up for class and do my best. Looking back, I appreciate that my parents made me pay my own way. It may have irritated me a little at the time, but it made me take school more seriously. If I was paying my way out of my pocket, there's no way I was going to stay out late and drink too much and miss class in the morning.

Eventually I ended up dropping out of college—because I became highly successful in helping people with their retirement plans. While I was building my practice, I got to the point where I was making more money than the college professors. I had several business classes where the professor stood there in front of the class and said things that I knew weren't true. I was out in the real world working in the investment arena. I asked myself why in the world was I going to continue to pay my own money to an institution that was teaching me things that I knew were incorrect or inaccurate? I had entered college with the intention of getting a good job after graduation, but I was fortunate to already have a good job and a wonderful career in front of me.

So I made the decision, much to the disappointment of my mother in particular, that I was going drop out. I wasn't going to complete the course load for the finance degree. I'm about a semester or two away from the four-year degree. The way I looked at it was that I'd gone to college to launch a good career. Three years into college, I had a good job; I had an established career that I was good at and that I really enjoyed. College had served its purpose.

Best Dollar We Never Spent

When my wife, Colleen, and I married, we bought a little condo, because we didn't want to rent. We saved up enough money for a down payment. When we moved into the condo, we took an approach of "let's take half of our combined income and put it into investments for our future"—our next house, or our retirement. So we covered boxes with tablecloths to make end tables. We didn't have a garbage can in the kitchen, and it used to drive my mother crazy. We would go to the grocery store and ask for paper bags, and each week we would use a new paper bag as the garbage can.

"Matt, you guys have jobs," my mother said. "Why don't you go buy a garbage can?"

"Mom, I'll get one eventually," I told her. I could see she was irritated. "It's just not a priority right now. We're saving half our money. We just don't have the money to buy a new garbage can." In reality we did have enough for a new garbage can and plenty of other items, but we had other priorities and we were beginning with the end in mind.

Eventually we acquired actual furniture and got rid of the boxes—and even the paper bags. But we sacrificed and cut corners. Today, we make more money than we can spend. We don't have to live the way we did then, but that mentality continues. We still cut coupons. We still turn off lights when we leave the room. I don't know why anyone wouldn't.

I suppose we could have splurged for that garbage can. We might even have found one for a dollar at a thrift shop. But the money that we set aside and saved was how we were able to start Strategic Wealth Designers, back in 2002. We put part of our savings into retirement plans, and the rest we invested in our business. The business today is worth millions, and that dollar, because it represents a portion of the startup cost, now represents a relative portion of the company's worth. We parlayed it into greater things down the road. We seized the opportunity instead of losing it.

Lost Opportunity Cost

When you enter a store and purchase something that you don't need, what does it cost you? Most would say the answer to that question depends on the price of the item. If you are analytical, you might ask, "Well, how much did it cost, and how much time was lost buying it?" Maybe you'll add the cost of the gas you used in driving back and forth from the store. Knowing how much the item cost, how much money you lost in time, and how much you spent on gas is a good start, but you are leaving out the most expensive variable. What could you have done with the money that you chose to spend on the item? What could you have earned, on the money you just spent, if you hadn't gone to the store and spent it unwisely to begin with?

It is estimated that an individual will lose between ten and twenty-million dollars during his or her lifetime by paying unnecessary fees, taxes, and expenses. The majority of this lost wealth comes from a little understood and often ignored concept called lost opportunity cost, or LOC. When you understand how LOC works, you will have a new way of looking at your finances and your money decisions.

HOW MUCH DOES LOST OPPORTUNITY COST?

Let's take a closer look at just what is involved in the concept of lost opportunity cost.

Suppose you bought an item that cost $1,000 after sales tax. The first step is to determine how much you had to earn to buy the item. In other words, how much gross income did you generate before income taxes to buy the item? If you are like most people, you earned $2,000 in order to have the $1,000 to spend. Most people are in a 50 percent tax bracket whether they know it or not. So, the $1,000 item is really a $2,000 gross income expense.

It gets worse, much worse. When you look at what you could have done with your $2,000 instead of spending it, you'll be amazed. Let's say you are thirty-five years old and you plan on retiring at age sixty-five. If you had invested the $2,000 and earned a 10 percent, tax free return each year, your $2,000 would have blossomed into almost $35,000!

Say you bought a new iPad, not because you need it, but because it's cool; or a new TV for a seldom-used room; or a new dress, for no reason other than because it was on sale; or a new bedroom set, not because yours was falling apart, but only because you visited the new furniture store in town and just had to have it; or whatever. How do you feel about that purchase now? Talk about buyer's remorse!

My point in this example is not to make you feel badly about spending your money. After all, what good is money if we can't spend and enjoy it? The purpose of sharing this with you is to help you understand the impact of LOC on your spending habits. I am not talking about whether you should buy a new TV or not; if the old one needs to be replaced, then by all means, get a new one.

The larger issue is the fact that, every year, you are more than likely spending a lot more than $2,000 simply because of bad financial advice. If we use the same rate of return from the example above, but instead we say that every year you are going to buy the $1,000 item that you had to earn $2,000 to get, the LOC over the same thirty-year period becomes almost $362,000.

Now, think for a moment about how much money you spend every year on insurance, taxes, and investment contributions. If you are thirty-five years old or older and you are earning $100,000, chances are that, after your mortgage, car loans, retirement contributions, taxes, and insurance premiums, you are left with between $10,000 and $30,000 per year to spend on the rest of the things you need or want, such as food, vacations, clothes, gifts, charity, entertainment, etc. (If your household earns $50,000, cut those figures in half; if your household earns $500,000, multiply them by five.)

Chances are, on January 1 each year, between 70 and 90 percent of all the money you are going to earn over the next year is already spoken for. Let's say, for example, it is just 80 percent or $80,000. What if you're doing a few things wrong with your investments or insurance? What if you are paying too much in taxes? How much is being lost?

Maybe you are paying out, to the various sources I mentioned, as little as $10,000 too much. The LOC on that $10,000 becomes a $6,151,616 loss when compounded every year for thirty years. That assumes the cost never goes up, meaning there is never any inflation added in. If we average an annual increase of just 4 percent inflation to the $10,000 that is being lost today, your LOC becomes almost $8,000,000 in thirty years.

To take this concept of LOC a step further, you have to look at what you would do with the $8,000,000 at age sixty-five. Would you spend it all or take an income stream? Most would take an income stream. What if you earned a 5 percent income stream for another thirty years before you passed away at age ninety-five? Leaving the original $8,000,000, you would have earned another $12,000,000 in interest. Assuming you lived on the $400,000 income that was generated each year, your total LOC over your lifetime ended up being $20,000,000. Had you not taken the 5 percent as income each year and instead reinvested the earnings, your $8,000,000 would have become $34,575,539 at age ninety-five.

To bring this concept closer to home, let's look at a specific example. Let's look at investing in a mutual fund portfolio outside of your company's retirement plan. Why would someone do this? Maybe he has maxed out on what could go into the company's retirement plan, or he wants to retire before age fifty-nine years, six months. Whatever the reason, investors do that every day. I am not totally against the idea; however, most of those investors have no idea how much money they are forfeiting to LOC. The taxes that they pay on their gains each year have a LOC. The loads, annual management fees, and account fees all have an LOC associated with them. If we just focus on the taxes for a moment, you will realize how expensive making poor investment decisions can become. (On a side note, I am not talking about picking bad mutual funds; I am talking about the problem with the strategy, not the product.)

Let's assume you are putting $6,000 a year into a no-load mutual fund. If those funds were to grow by an average of 8 percent every year for thirty years, at the end you would have just over $734,000.

So, you feel pretty good because you saved a good deal of money over those thirty years and your contribution grew into a nice pile with which you can supplement your retirement. But what about the LOC? Consider the LOC on the tax that you had to pay each year because of your investment gains. Assuming you were in a tax bracket of 40 percent over those thirty years, you would have had to pay over $221,000 in taxes.

But that is not all. If you didn't have to pay the IRS these tax dollars each year, you could have invested them instead. Assuming you earned the same 8 percent of what you paid out in taxes each year, your $221,000 tax bill becomes a $448,000 LOC. So you invested a total of $180,000 ($6,000 x 30 years) and it cost you $448,000 in tax and LOC in order to accumulate $734,000. This is the equivalent of earning less than 2 percent on your money.

Chances are that, right now, you are either paying too much for your insurance premiums or you have a mortgage that is not the right type, or you are investing long-term money into taxable accounts. Any and all of those mistakes could be costing you millions of dollars in LOC. Lost opportunities could be costing you a prosperous retirement. It's time to get back on track.

CHAPTER 8

STOP FOLLOWING THE HERD

Back in 2008, as the market was plunging 39 percent, I overheard a conversation that spoke volumes about the risk of listening to people who might not have your best interests at heart. I was in the cafeteria of the building in Lexington where our satellite office shares space with others in the financial services industry. As stocks took a dive, people were panicking. It was as if the world were ending. I went to the cafeteria for some coffee, and I heard two advisors talking. Neither knew me—I was new in the building at that time.

"It's just awful," one advisor said. "Our clients are calling right and left. They're panicking. Everybody wants to sell."

"Ours, too," the other advisor commiserated. "They all want to get out of the market. They want to move to cash."

"Can't let them do it," the first said. "We can't make money that way. No commissions in cash."

"We've got to keep 'em believing it'll be okay," said the second, "that it'll all be better soon, and they shouldn't be so foolish to bail out of their mutual funds."

"So how's your own portfolio?" the first asked the second, as they parted.

"Mine? I took all my money out of the market months ago." The other laughed. "Uh huh, so did I."

That is indeed how a lot of advisors view the client—as a number. As a means to a commission. Advisors need money to pay their mortgages and bills and send their kids to college. The truth would not serve them well. They're not going to recommend that you pay them less. There are exceptions to that rule, but that's how many advisors operate.

Bad Advice Abounds

We get a lot of bad advice from people. A high percentage of them are not going to have a successful retirement because they haven't saved enough. That means that if you're asking your friends and family for advice, your odds are slim that you will get good guidance. Or maybe the information they give you would be correct for them, but it doesn't necessarily mean that it would apply to your situation.

Sometimes people tell me, "I've got a really wealthy uncle who does just fine and he manages all of his money on his own. He tells me, 'Who needs a financial planner? Just do it on your own.'" And that might work for the rich uncle who has forty or fifty hours a week to do his own research and actually has a knack and enjoys trying to pick and choose the right stocks or bonds to invest in. But the truth is most people can't do that on their own.

Your rich uncle may have succeeded, but that doesn't mean you will. What helped him gain wealth and success in years past might not help the investor of today. The markets and the economy are different than they were over the last ten, twenty, and thirty years. On the other hand, be careful that you don't go to a poor uncle for advice, either. Some people get a college degree and think they know a lot. Perhaps they do, in something or other, but the reality is many don't know a thing about the world of finance and investments.

There's a load of bad information out there, and it is spread for a variety of reasons. Some of it is coming from financial advisors who have a hidden agenda; they want to sell you the highest commission product or the highest fee product.

At Strategic Wealth Designers, we don't necessarily do what's popular, but we do what's right. In our educational events and news appearances, we don't necessarily say all the things people are hoping to hear, but we certainly will share with them some information that they need to know. If you want to be successful, you can't follow the herd.

You must do things differently, because the great majority of people get it wrong. Don't be like everybody else. You want to be in the minority. You want to be the exception to the rule.You can't trust the advice of friends and family and acquaintances, because most all are on the wrong path. They're not qualified to be your guide. If you go to the bank for advice, you will likely hear what is in the best interests of the bank. Same with a stock brokerage firm. Someone may have a quota or be going for a bonus. The banks don't really have attractive solutions right now that will work for retirees. CDs are paying 1 percent or less. If you ask for something better, you'll be introduced to "financial advisors," who might have little experience. They might not really know a whole lot. They just know they're supposed to sell these mutual funds to whoever comes along and asks for something better than a CD. That way the bank can keep your money in-house and they continue to profit via the com- mission and fees that the mutual fund will generate. It's a rigged game. And some people play it with blind faith, because they like that solid feel of bricks and mortar, and the tellers might even know their names. That doesn't mean the bank has the market cornered on the best available investment vehicles.

The advisors at the bank or the large brokerage can only recommend certain things—and what they can recommend is what the institution allows them to talk about. And what they're allowed to talk about many times, are the things that generate the most money. Typically, the bank advisors don't have a full complement of products or strategies that they can use. They have a limited number of investments that they can recommend to you.

And of course they're not going to speak positively about those things that they can't recommend to you. If you go to a Ford dealership and you're looking at a truck, what would you expect as a response if you asked the salesperson, "How do you like that new Chevy?" The Ford dealership is not going to say anything positive about the Chevy. It sells Fords. So the salesperson is going to talk about all the reasons that you don't want to buy a Chevy but instead want to buy a Ford. It's the same dynamic when you go to a broker to ask about investments. You will hear all the reasons that you don't want your money in a safer position, or you will be told that you need to diversify and you need to buy these mutual funds. Nothing surprising there: That's the business they're in.

People are somehow savvy enough to understand that the auto dealerships are delivering a spiel. But somehow that doesn't click for them when they walk into the bank or the brokerage firm. They don't make that connection, even if they're intelligent, sophisticated people. It seems as if there's an aura of authority around the banker, or around anyone who is sitting behind a desk talking about finances. Following the herd is hardly a good investment strategy, yet I'm amazed at how many people I've met who use nothing more than a perception of what's hot and what's not to make their investment decisions. Such herd mentality led to the dot-com bubble after 1999. Investors knew that such a rapid rise in values was unprecedented and dangerous, yet they fueled the fire and bought the stocks anyway. Wealth vanished.

Lessons from the Past

People typically learn what they know about investing from experience. Many advisors and investors, especially those approaching retirement age, remember the stock market as it was in the 1980s and 90s, when diversification strategies, "staying the course," and investing for the long run actually worked for the majority of people. Back then, most people made their money back within a few years after a volatile period in the market.

Despite record highs in the stock market, we are in a very unstable economic atmosphere and there is little indication we'll be coming out of it anytime soon. You need an advisor who has a thorough historical perspective on the markets. You should also try to learn as much about market history as you can as it will better prepare you to recognize questionable advice when you hear it.

All investment advisors are not created equal. Unfortunately, most people do not realize that a financial advisor's background, training, and the goals of his or her current employer are going to greatly influence the investment advice given. It only makes sense, right? But the advice you get can be seriously flawed if that advisor is not looking out for your best interests, not mindful of the history of the market, not actively watching current and emerging trends, and not adjusting the investment plans of his or her clients accordingly.

One of the biggest mistakes investors make is getting on the computer and searching the vast and lawless reaches of the Internet for investment strategies and ideas. Searching for investment advice online will yield countless hits, some of which will be accurate but most will not. It's not that the information is inherently flawed, necessarily, but it is likely to be of little or no use to you because it is not taking into consideration your current situation, your investment goals, or even the current state of the market. You may be sifting through advice that is years old.

You have to realize that anyone can have a webpage on which they can say just about whatever they want. Similarly, it will also be necessary for you to filter out the noise of our twenty-four seven news cycle, which tends toward sensationalism and can make investors feel unduly anxious. It's important not to let your emotions, or the emotions of others, guide your investment decisions.

It has been said that there is safety in numbers, but you don't want to find out, after it's too late, that the expression does not apply to your retirement. Be wary of the words coming from a lazy advisor, the Internet, or a family friend. They may be dispensing the outdated strategies of yesteryear.

Riding the Roller Coaster

Just following the market news can feel as if you are riding a roller coaster. Investing in the market will subject you to wild swings of emotion. If you look at a line graph of the stock market's performance for any given period of time, it will certainly look like a roller coaster track—highs and lows, peaks and dips, followed by more of the same.

To give you some perspective on what all of those rises and falls mean, let's take a closer look at the history of the stock market and the U.S. economy. It will give you a better understanding of the cyclical nature of the market and help you make better decisions for your financial future.

I firmly believe the adage that those who don't know history are destined to repeat it. The stock market clearly runs on certain predictable cycles. Although we can't pinpoint the day that a major change will ensue, we can predict the direction of the cycle or trend that we are in.

The years 1930–48 were a dismal time for most investors. The effects of the collapse of the U.S. stock market were felt around the world. Unemployment, low commodity prices, significant reductions in foreign trade, a halt in consumer spending, and widespread price declines led to a financial meltdown. Chances are, if you put a dollar in the market in 1930, you had to wait until 1948 just to earn that dollar back.

It was eighteen years of little to no growth. We now know this time as the Great Depression.

The next cycle was 1948–66. The United States had prevailed in World War II, the soldiers came home, the nation celebrated, and U.S. manufacturing skyrocketed. Almost everything in the country was produced within its borders, and pent-up consumer demand for necessities and luxury items alike ensured an economic boom. It was a great time for most investors.

Then came 1966–82. During that cycle, we had concerns about rising inflation, unstable interest rates, out-of-control oil and gas prices, and major political unrest. We were involved in a very unpopular war, and we did not know how or when it was going to end and we had no way of paying for it other than going into debt. Some people will think that this scenario sounds as if I'm talking about the world today, but this is looking back nearly half a century. It was a bad period for most investors. Another sixteen years with no growth in the stock market.

Then, from 1982 to 2000, we had the greatest bull market we had ever seen. During the last five years of that period, we saw the meteoric rise of the dot-com bubble. A lot of people made a lot of money very quickly. It was an extremely good time to be an investor.

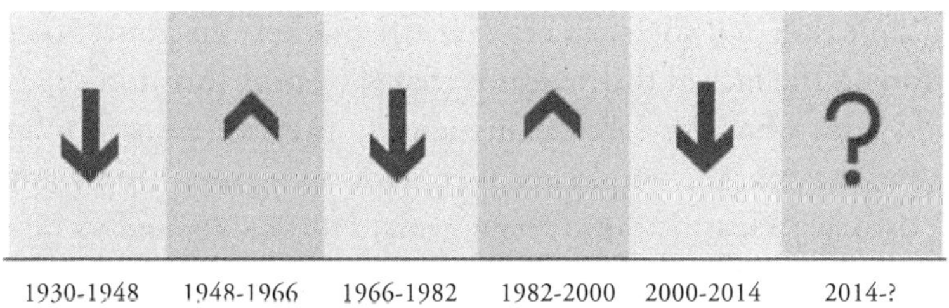

The next period began in 2000 with the dot com bubble burst and subsequent market crash, the September 11, 2011 terrorist attacks followed by the start of wars in Afghanistan and Iraq, hurricane Katrina and the financial crisis in 2008. These major world events as well as a host of other minor happenings led to the market being essentially flat until 2014.

Looking at the years 2014 to today, the market has been up over that period. You may have noticed that these cycles take anywhere from fourteen to eighteen years to work themselves out, so you might conclude that the cycle we're in is far from over. If you and I were to talk again in 2028 or 30, what do you think we'd say about our most recent investment cycle? Do you think we'll say it was a great time to be an investor and that we made a lot of money? Or do you think we'll look back and say the entire period was awful? No one knows for sure, but history tells us when the market goes down it eventually comes back- and that seems to be the cycle we're in now.

I am not pretending to be able to predict the future. Some of you, however, may be working with advisors who believe they can. During past economic downturns, you may have heard comments such as "Just sit tight, we'll wait until you get back to even pretty soon, then we'll make changes." If they are saying things like that, they are really saying loud and clear that they do not understand the history of the market.

If such advisors profess to be able to predict the future and when their clients will get their money back, then why didn't they tell their clients that the market was going to go down? The fact of the matter is that they probably don't have any idea what they are talking about. They were just hoping that the market would recover within two or three years. History is clear: It takes seven years, on average, and as long as eighteen, to get back to even.

During the Great Depression in the 1930s, the market went down, edged up and fell, repeatedly- and each time it sank it hit a new low. Many investors sat tight and hoped everything would work out for them. By the time the market hit rock bottom, they had lost on average 89.5 percent of their account values. It took them eighteen years to recover from that event and even longer if you factor in inflation.

I'm not saying it will get that bad again, but history does have a way of repeating itself. It's no time to panic, but neither do you want to bury your head in the sand and hope all will be well. Investors who try that have found that the strategy doesn't serve them well. If you have assets worth protecting, now is the time to put a safety net under your accounts. You don't want to risk losing what you worked so hard to gain.

INVESTING DOESN'T HAVE TO BE A ROLLER COASTER RIDE!

Chapter 9
Planning for Prosperity

Is a Will the Way?

If you die without a will, what happens to your estate depends upon the state you lived in. Estate planning is different in all fifty states. Each has its own set of rules. In some states, everyone who passes away has a will. If you don't have one that you created yourself, the state gives it to you. But it's not one that anybody would ever want. If you have any assets at all, you want your own will.

A common belief is that if you're married and pass away, your spouse inherits everything. In some states that's true, but in others it does not necessarily work that way. Basically, the surviving spouse in some states gets half of the assets. Then there is a pecking order among other family members for the other half. The spouse gets half. Brothers and sisters get a portion, as do the parents, if they're alive. In other states, passing away without a will just means there can be an enormous fight over what you have, and the case will be tied up in the courts for however long those involved want to fight over it. Usually nobody wins except for the attorneys whom you need to hire to go through what's called probate to have your estate closed out. The process sucks the value out of the estate—money that could have gone to so many better purposes.

A lot of times people will have a will, but it may not have been updated in fifteen years. Our advisors know enough to be helpful, but these cases must be referred to a qualified attorney. I usually recommend that you work with an attorney who is an estate planning specialist. You don't want somebody who does an occasional will or trust here and there. You want to deal with an attorney who is licensed in your state. You need somebody that knows the local laws.

Power of Attorney

There are two types of powers of attorney. You can grant medical power of attorney, which says in effect, "If I become incapacitated, this person has the authority to make decisions regarding my health care." And you can grant financial power of attorney, so that your investments and assets can be tapped to take care of your obligation. Many people have what's called a powerless power of attorney—meaning that whoever is designated to have power of attorney—typically, a spouse or family member—does not also have financial rights. That creates problems. If you don't have the financial provisions in a power of attorney, you can't access money to pay for bills or medication or repairs. Unless investment accounts are in your name, too, you can't withdraw money.

Living Wills

Medical power of attorney usually is in coordination with a living will. A will specifies what happens upon your death; a living will specifies your desires if you are still alive but, in a coma or unable to communicate or make decisions.

The living will just says what you would want to have happen if you were to become incapacitated and unable to make decisions on your own. A living will relieves the family of having to decide whether their loved one should stay on life support for years—or be allowed to die if there's no improvement in condition within a certain period of time. That's a tough place to put your family, and a living will settles the matter. A lot of times if there's no living will, people will argue both sides. They'll say, "No, no, no, Uncle Fred wouldn't have wanted to live in a coma." Other family members maintain the opposite: "We must do what we can. If there's even a 1 percent chance he can get better, he wouldn't want us to turn off the life support."

The living will avoids that dispute by spelling out what *you* want. That way there are no guesses, and nobody has to live with con- sequences of those decisions. You decide up front what you would want to have happen if you ever found yourself in that situation.

Update Your Beneficiaries

Sometimes people get divorced or they get remarried, and they've never changed the beneficiaries on their accounts. It happens: The husband passes away, and rather than the new spouse getting the money, the ex-wife gets it all. The judge's hands are tied. If the account owner never made the change in beneficiaries, there's no way of undoing that. It's final.

I bring that issue up with clients during the planning process, making sure all such documents are updated. Some people just forget. They get busy with other things in their lives. It's not top of mind for them. We always review and make sure that, if something were to happen to them, their money would go to the people or the places where they want it to go

Danger of Procrastinating

Estate planning is not a whole lot of fun to talk about. It's not fun to consider what you'd like to have happen if you were in a coma or killed in a plane crash. You come face to face with your own mortality.

Still, it's not as if you have to talk about such considerations daily. Once you have gone through the planning process and a professional has drawn up the papers and you have signed them, you're done. You do an update every five or ten years, or whenever you have a significant change in life such as a divorce or a marriage, or the birth of a child, or the death of a beneficiary. You take care of matters and then file the papers away again. It's not fun, but sometimes you have to go to the doctor and take the medicine. Whether you like it or not, it's something you have to do.

It's easy to procrastinate. You could spend your whole life procrastinating until it's too late. We tend to think it's other people who get killed in car crashes, or who fall off ladders, or who contract a fatal disease. It's a sad refrain: "I never thought it would happen to me." We're hard-wired to believe bad things won't come to us. If you truly recognized what potentially could happen to you during the course of a day, you would never get out of bed.

Nonetheless, most people do acknowledge that there are risks involved whenever they get up and leave the house—or even when they stay home. They see the travails that others endure, and that helps to dispel the attitude of "I'll get around to it someday." That is what motivates them to take action.

Setting up a Trust

Almost every attorney who does estate planning will recommend that you start a trust for your heirs, as opposed to just a will and standard planning. What are the situations in which it's wise to have a trust? I'm not an attorney, but I don't think everybody needs one. Trusts are helpful, but they can also be expensive.

If you have a pretty basic situation, you might not need a trust. This is a basic situation: You married your high school sweetheart, you had two kids, you have always lived in the same state, and you worked no more than a couple of jobs. All of your property is in one state—maybe two, if you have a vacation home. Your sons-in-law or your daughters-in-law are good, upstanding citizens who love your kids. And your grandkids are wonderful. If so, then you might not need a trust.

A trust helps you control your money after you're gone. That's a way of looking at it. When you die, the will distributes your assets to the people and the places you designate. If you have a trust, it's a mechanism to help you continue to control the money from the grave. You can still stipulate how the money is handled.

Instead of giving your daughter, who has a spending problem, $1,000,000 when you pass away, maybe you give her $30,000 a year for as long as she lives. Maybe she can take out more if she gets married, or a lump sum once her child is old enough to go to college, as long as that money is going to be spent on higher education.

You can basically stipulate anything that you can think of to control the money from the grave. If you have a situation where you have a child or beneficiaries who have spending problems, addictions, or are married to an abusive spouse, a trust can limit and direct the distribution of finances. If you have a child with special needs, you can set money aside for lifelong care.

Maybe you have a complex situation where you have been married three times and have kids with two or three different people, and you have property in fifteen states. A will probably isn't going to do the job. You're going to need more advanced estate planning. Also, having a trust can in some cases help you avoid estate taxes. In such cases, a trust makes sense, but many people with simpler issues should carefully weigh the cost of setting up a trust against the benefits. They're an important element in retirement planning, but they aren't for everyone.

Charitable Giving

Retirees often are concerned about how to effectively leave money to charity without being taxed so heavily. You can do that with a trust or without a trust. You can take money out of your accounts while you're living, give it away to charity, and get that tax deduction for it. You can now withdraw money from an IRA and give it directly to a charity, and that's not a taxable event.

There are many ways trusts can be used for charitable giving in estate planning. Typically where you have the trust, say a charitable remainder trust, you put money aside and basically give up access to it. You might live on the interest that the assets will produce, but then when you pass away, 100 percent of that money bypasses your estate and goes directly to the charity that you designated. No estate taxes are due.

When you are able to effectively distribute your money to charity, you are retaining control over your money. Instead of giving it to the government to decide whom it wants to give the money, you decide. You decide what good gets done with your life's savings.

Confidence Comes From Understanding

I believe it is important that you see precisely what is happening with your money. The more that people understand that, the more likely they will be to relax and enjoy themselves. If you don't really understand what's happening, you may feel as if you have to hoard and can't do anything. You can't take the trip. You feel you can't give the money to your grandkid for a college education. You're paralyzed by the unknown—by the fear of running out of money.

But when you can clearly grasp your financial situation, then you feel more comfortable spending and enjoying your money, doing the things that you want to do. That's really what it's all about. That's why you worked all those years and set money aside—to enjoy what it could bring to you in the future.

Getting Started

How to Choose an Expert Advisor

Every so often, someone will ask me, "Why do I need an investment advisor? Can't I get all the information and advice I need from the Internet?" If you can, maybe you don't need an advisor. But the truth is, most people can't do that. There is so much information on the Web that, yes, it can be a great resource with which to do research. If you're talking with an advisor and you don't understand certain terms or phrases, you can certainly get online and research them. But investors must understand that while there's a lot of information out there, there are also a lot of misconceptions and misinformation out there, too. You have to be very, very careful about the information you read online. I heard a speaker once say that if we looked to the TV news to get all of our information about airplanes, we would probably believe that all airplanes that take off either crash or land in a river. Sure, some planes crash and some occasionally land in a river, but that doesn't mean that all of them do. And that's the nature of information on the Internet. You might hear or read something that's good for the person giving that information, but it might not be good for your situation.

If you are interviewing advisors, you should ask how they are going to be paid, and ask if they can provide you with a wealth management agreement that you can review and both of you will sign if you engage that advisor. I also recommend that you ask for references and call those references. Any advisor should have several clients who have given them permission to use their name. Research and due diligence of this sort allows individuals to do a great job of protecting themselves.

Usually when we meet with somebody for the first time, we're trying to see if we can help them out in some way—or not, because we can't help everybody. So the first meeting is trying to determine if there is any value we can bring. We don't take a cookie-cutter approach. Life experiences and needs are vastly different, and sometimes when we meet people for the first time they have a thorn in their side, a rock in their shoe. They have a burning issue to fix. Other clients just want an overall plan, nothing urgent. They want to know where they're going and how they're going to get there. When we sit down to talk, there is no set agenda. We just want to get to know each other better. We are trying to see if this person needs our help.

A lot of investors paint all financial advisors with the same brush. They think that every advisor has the same advice and the same products, and that there really isn't any difference from one to the other. Many think that all advisors are held to a high standard of fiduciary responsibility and that they're always acting in the client's best interest. You may even play golf with your advisor, or go to the same church, or maybe your kids are friends and go to the same school. You may think your advisor is a great person, and they very well may be. But business is business, and there are many factors at play that influence how an advisor does the job.

There are things you should know, and questions you should ask, to ensure that you have an investment advisor who is helping you, rather than preventing you, from securing the best retirement you possibly can.

Beware of Skewed Advice

Advisors will always give advice based on their background and the priorities of their firm. Insurance agents are far more likely to want to sell life insurance or annuities to their clients, because that's their business. Stockbrokers are typically going to stocks, bonds and mutual funds because that's how they make their money. And, of course, if your advisor is a representative of a bank, they're likely going to shade their recommendations to fixed income vehicles like CD's or other bank sponsored products. The advice you get is always skewed by the type of individual you're talking to and by the type of firm he or she represents. That's why you have to take the time to ask questions. You only get one shot at getting your retirement right, and it is up to you to make sure you're getting the correct advice that's going to be suitable for you and your situation.

SIX QUESTIONS TO ASK YOUR FINANCIAL ADVISOR

What makes you an expert? How successful are you?

You have to ask your advisor how they think they'll be able to help you and how successful they are at their job. You might have an advisor with an alphabet of letters behind his or her name, but you need to find out how much real world experience he has in helping retirees and pre-retirees. There's a big difference between studying in a book how to be a financial advisor and actually applying those methods and experiencing what works and what doesn't work. It's kind of like a doctor who reads all the medical books and knows how to perform the surgery but hasn't actually done it. You want to find out what makes your current advisor an expert and how successful they are.

The second part of that question is obviously very important. You want to find out how many clients the advisor has, how much experience they have in dealing with bull and bear markets, and how many clients they have helped transition from working into retirement.

Are you a registered representative, or an investment advisor representative?

Those two titles might sound similar, but there's a big difference in the type of advice you're going to get. Many people think all advisors do what's in the best interest of their clients. I certainly wish it was that way, but it's not.

This is a question of to whom or what the advisor has a fiduciary responsibility. It's an important concept to understand. Not all financial advisors have an obligation—a fiduciary responsibility—to look out for you and do what's best for your investments and your retirement.

If you currently work with an advisor from one of the large firms, and on his or her business card it says, "registered representative," that means the advisor has a fiduciary responsibility to the firm. Instead of being obligated to put their clients' interests ahead of their own, registered representative are expected to deal *fairly* with their clients and adhere to a lower standard of legal care, known as the suitability doctrine. This doctrine requires a registered representative to know their client's financial situation well enough to recommend investments that are considered *suitable* for that particular client. Some firms have dually registered representatives who can act in both capacities, but it's important to ask questions and understand which hat they're wearing.

To emphasize the fact that they work in the firm's best interest, not the client's, let me give you an example of what would happen if an investor gets into some sort of conflict with a registered representative and they end up in court. Let's say the judge asks the advisor, "Why did you recommend this product when this other product would have been better for your client?" A legitimate response for a registered representative would be, "I sold this other product because that's what makes my firm the most money. I'm a W2 employee of that firm, and that's what I have to do." That's a fully acceptable answer in that situation as long as the products are deemed suitable for the client. Why? It's acceptable because, as a paid employee of the firm, the advisor's obligation is to sell products and make money for the firm. That's what he or she is legally contracted to do. Registered representatives are not legally obligated to save money for investors at the expense of their employer. The firm dictates what products, services and strategies a registered representative can and can't recommend to clients. That's why these firms can have quotas for a certain amount of mutual funds or certain products that the advisors have to sell, regardless of whether it's in the client's best interest. How do I know this? I used to be a registered representative at one of the large firms. Once I realized how things operated there, I left to start my own company. Now, I don't have quotas or a manager looking over my shoulder telling me to sell products instead of helping people build and enjoy their retirement.

On the other hand, you could work with someone like me, who is part of a registered investment advisory firm. Our firm is a Registered Investment Advisors (RIA), and our advisors are known as Investment Advisor Representatives (IARs). We, unlike registered representatives, have a fiduciary responsibility to our clients. Let's go back to the same scenario I used a moment ago, but instead of a registered representative, we have an advisor who is an IAR and registered with a registered investment advisory firm. If that advisor were to recommend a product that was not in the best interest of the client—let's say he sold a product that would line his pockets with additional compensation and commission, but not necessarily improve the retirement portfolio of the client—he could potentially lose his license, have to pay fines, and, depending on how severe the offense, go to jail.

The good news is that Congress is working on financial reform regulations. The legislation would require stockbrokers, insurance agents, and other financial advisors to have the same fiduciary responsibility standard that RIAs have. All of the big brokerage firms are fighting this, and they have a lot of money and some powerful lobbyists with which to do so. They don't want the laws to change, because if they do, their advisors are going to have to start acting in the clients' best interest, not in the firms' best interest. And, of course, that would bring down their profits and revenue.

When advisors align themselves to act in the best interest of the client, this will typically lead to lower fees because they are not going to be motivated by commission-based earnings. And fees, as this book has amply explained, can make a big difference in whether you will enjoy a successful retirement.

How have you performed over the last ten years?

I've been in the industry since 1997, but I've also been a student of the markets, and it is very important to find out how an advisor has performed over the last ten years. It is common for me to meet people whose investments haven't gone anywhere for eight, nine, even a dozen years. Almost every day, people tell me they've watched an investment go up and down for a decade without earning anything. If it takes you five, ten, or fifteen years to recover from a bear market, you have never really recovered, because you have wasted all that time making your money back when you could have been building upon it from the start. You are that many years older and closer to retirement, if you're not already in it, and inflation has rendered your money unable to purchase what it would have bought when the bear market began.

I encourage you not to buy into the "I never saw it coming" excuse. In 2008, a lot of investors lost money. When they called their advisors, they heard this line: "Everybody's losing money. Nobody saw this coming." I don't buy that. You don't care about everybody else losing money; you care about your own money and your retirement. A good advisor who was paying attention to what was happening in the U.S. economy should have seen it coming. After all, it is the advisor's job to see it coming. When the stock market is growing, it's very easy for an advisor to make his clients money; but making your clients money even when the stock market is going down is what separates the professionals from the amateurs.

Are you open to change?
How do you keep up on new strategies?

There are advisors out there who still follow strategies that worked very well back in the 1980s and '90s. Unfortunately, the economy we're in now is not the same, and it's not going to be that way again anytime soon. Find out what your advisor is doing to stay abreast of the changes that are going on in the industry and economy. Are they well versed, or do they use a cookie-cutter approach?

Some advisors are trained to do only mutual funds all the time, or maybe they take the approach that life insurance is best all the time. It might be good for them, if they only need to know one product or two products. They can talk about them and sound well educated, but that's not going to be good enough. They have to recognize and adapt to change. If an advisor hasn't changed his approach in the past three to five years, chances are he is going to lose a lot of clients, or a lot of those clients are going to struggle during retirement.

What direction do you think the country is headed?

This nation faces undeniable challenges, and things going on in Washington and around the country regarding the economy will dramatically influence the direction of the stock market, interest rates, the value of the dollar, and your retirement savings. You must find out how your advisor thinks these concerns will impact the country and the economy.

We have a national debt of over twenty-two trillion dollars and growing rapidly. If the economy continues to grow, the debt will likely stabilize or get smaller; but if there's no growth it might get worse. That's not even considering our unfunded liabilities. David Walker, the former U.S. comptroller, recently spoke at great length about the fact that the unfunded liabilities of Medicare, Medicaid, and Social Security will equal about fifty-trillion dollars by 2050.

So, by the year 2050, just those three things—not including national defense, education spending or anything else—will add fifty-trillion dollars in debt. And that number does not include spending for national health care.

We are going to have to increase taxes, and it will impact every- body's spendable dollars, including those for retirement. Record low unemployment rates complicates the prospect for long term retail growth as companies struggle to find good workers to fill their open positions. The real estate market continues to feel pressure, and that complicates the problem of unemployment and retail growth. This is all interrelated.

Ask your advisor how these matters will impact your retirement dollars. You have to work hard to earn a reasonable return in these times, but it's still possible and it's certainly needed. Unless you have accumulated all the money you're ever going to need to last you the rest of your life, you still have to grow the money you have. My clients want to see it grow in a safe manner, and we have a variety of ways that you can do that.

Find out how your advisor proposes to help your money grow. If he tells you not to worry because he diversified your investments to protect you, here is the full Warren Buffett quote that I mentioned early in this book:

"Taking a diversified approach with your money means that you really don't know what's going to happen. Taking a diversified approach really is protection against ignorance, and it makes little sense if you know what you're doing. Advisors will recommend diversification to protect you against their ignorance."

The quote is not meant to offend anyone. If you invest your money on your own in your 401K or your IRA and you don't know everything that a professional might know, then go ahead and diversify. Diversification can make sense if you really don't know what you're doing.

A 20-Point Checklist for your Retirement

Let's look at twenty of the most important things you can do to make sure you're prepared to transition to retirement. It's an exciting time, but retiring also can be scary.

What should be a time of happiness or joy can turn highly stressful without proper planning.

Most people relish the prospect of retiring, but some people struggle with it. Leaders and managers have felt important in their careers. People came to them with questions. And then they retire and that stops. To fill that void, they may find it helpful to get involved in a charity or take a leadership position within their homeowner's association.

That's just one of many pitfalls that retirees might not see coming. You quickly realize how many things that you need to evaluate. You need to plan well, so that what should be a thriving time in your golden years doesn't become disappointing to you. Retirement should be exciting. It shouldn't be stressful.

That's why we put together this 20-point retirement checklist. Over the years we have helped hundreds of clients make the transition from working into retirement. These are the most common questions that come up.

Even on your first day of retirement, you may wonder: Where's the money? If you've been working for thirty or forty years, you're used to getting paid every other week or twice a month, and all of a sudden you go into retirement and that's it. Maybe you have a pension plan, but a lot of times those take a month or two before the money flows to you. Social Security payments sometimes are late in getting processed, so the situation can feel scary: "What am I going to do for income while I'm going through this transition period?"

Usually what we recommend is this: If you're used to getting paid twice a month, we can set up a retirement plan where you get money deposited into your account twice a month. Try to make things resemble the way they were when you were working. It helps to alleviate stress.

This checklist could be helpful not only if you are retiring this year but if you have several years before you retire. Of course, the earlier you start planning, the better off you typically will be. You have more time to get your ducks in a row.

1. Get out of debt

The first thing that we almost always recommend before somebody officially retires is to eliminate or reduce debt. Sometimes it's all right to have a mortgage, but I prefer to see clients have their mortgage paid off at that point. Obviously, you can't have any significant credit card debt or high-interest debt or even car loans unless you have zero percent interest. You're going to have a reduction in income, typically, and you're not going to have as much monthly cash flow, so any debt will add to your stress.

2. Create an emergency cash reserve

The second thing that you definitely want to do is create an emergency cash reserve. Of course, this is true for anyone, not just retirees. Different advisors will recommend different amounts. Some will tell you that you need three months' worth of expenses in an easy-to-access account. Others will tell you six months. Some will say a year.

I like the six-month rule of thumb for money that you can get too quickly. Obviously, if you're retiring, you should have funds other than just this emergency cash reserve, but if you have a six-month cash reserve, you will have six months to deal with contingencies. If you need to remove money from different investments or take money out of an IRA, an emergency fund allows you plenty of time to make those arrangements.

When you're looking for a higher rate of return on your money, you have to either put it at risk or agree not to withdraw all of it for a certain amount of time. Whether you are doing risk or time, that money will not be immediately available, and you need to have money set aside for those emergencies that always come up. Someone gets sick or hurt. The roof gives out. A grandchild has a problem. You need emergency reserves.

3. Apply for financing before you retire

Even if you do not plan to use it, apply for financing before you retire. Let's say that you still have a mortgage but you want to get a lower interest rate or change the terms. Do that before you retire.

Obviously, the bank is more likely to give someone a loan who has a job and a steady income. So don't wait. Also, we often recommend establishing a home-equity line of credit even if you don't use it. Let's say your house is paid off. You should establish that credit line for emergencies. Most banks will charge you $50 a year to have that home equity line, but that's a good emergency fund.

Even if you are seventy-two and semiretired and feel that you will be turned down for a loan because of your age, take heart: The banks are not allowed to do that. That is against the law. You could be ninety-five years old. I know this is a concern for a lot of seniors, but the fact of the matter is, that is discrimination. Don't let that concern stop you from moving forward.

4. *Retire when it benefits you most*

Determine the best day to retire to maximize your employer benefits. This can make a big difference. Sometimes, people are forced into early retirement and don't get to choose the day. I understand that's sometimes the case, especially if there are economic concerns like corporate downsizing or cutbacks. But if you can, try to determine the best day to retire.

Say, for example, your company pays a profit-sharing bonus or an annual bonus and you have to be employed on the day that it is paid. You want to find that out. Don't assume that the year's bonus will be paid to you because you worked the whole year. If the company typically pays those bonuses in April and you want to retire on March 1, you might not get that bonus check.

Same thing if you have any additional retirement days coming to you. We work with a lot of government employees, and often they work one day into the next year, because they get their full vacation allocation for the year. Find out those types of things before you pick the date.

I recommend retiring in the spring or the summer if you can. Retirement requires adjustments and transition, and our clients who retire in the spring or in the summer tend to adapt better. In the winter, when it's cold you can't do as many things. People are a little grumpier when they're not seeing the sun. If you have to retire during the cold-weather months, I usually recommend that, within a week or two of retirement, you go somewhere warm. Travel to a place where you have long wanted to go, and celebrate.

5. *Anticipate changing expenses*

It's important to control your spending and identify additional expenditures you will have once you retire. There is a school of thought—and people repeat it to me—that when you retire, you don't need as much income as when you were working. Different studies and statistics say you will need 70 percent of your pre-retirement income, or 60 percent, or 80 percent. Actually, it depends on how lavish a lifestyle you want when you retire.

An example is travel expenses. During their working life, people often struggle and sacrifice. They don't go on lavish vacations because they need to put money aside to pay for expenses such as a college education for their children. But now that they have retired and the kids are raised, they tell me that they want to travel. They want to go to Europe every year or take a thirty-day cruise. Their income needs easily could be 100 percent of what they made before retiring. At the other end of the spectrum, some clients tell me, "If I just don't have to get up to go to work on Monday, I'll be happy. I don't need to travel. I don't need a lavish lifestyle. I don't need a new car every few years." They might need less income than they earned while working.

You do need to plan for the fact that when you retire, you will need to do something to fill all those hours that you previously spent at work, not to mention commuting. You could have sixty hours a week of time to do something new. Chances are you're not just going to sit on the couch. You're going to do something, and that of course is going to require money.

People believe they will spend less, and that's a major mistake they make as they head into retirement. They in fact will spend a lot of money during those hours that they used to be on the job. Even if you just want to plant a garden, you need to buy seeds and equipment, and it adds up. Some people work on classic or collector cars. Some people like to shop. You will be doing something with all those added hours, and that something likely will cost some money. Almost all of our retiring clients tell me that they don't want their monthly income to go down much at all. They want to maintain their lifestyle; otherwise, they'd just keep on working.

6. *Decide the lifestyle you want*

I'll sometimes ask couples, "What are you planning to do? Where are you going? Are you going to live in the house that you live in right now, or are you going to downsize?" A lot of people plan on downsizing, but many want to keep the big house so the grandkids will have a place to sleep over when they visit. "We don't want them to stay in the motel down the road," they'll say. Either way, make those decisions before you enter retirement.

7. *Evaluate your pension options*

Depending on the company, you could have numerous payout options under your pension plan. If something happens to you, does the money go to a spouse? If something happens to both of you, then what? You want to get information on those pension plan payout options early. Pension plans sometimes take awhile to either get rolled over or to get the income started, so don't wait until the 11th-hour. You want to give yourself plenty of time to make an educated decision.

8. *Calculate how long your money will last*

If you don't know how to do that, don't panic. We can work with you to determine how much money you will need, based on your expectations for retirement, and run an analysis to calculate how much money you will be able to draw from your nest egg so that it lasts as long as you do.

9. Tell your insurance agent you're retiring

This is a way of saving some money. Typically, your auto insurance premium will go down a little bit because you are no longer driving back and forth from work, so you don't have those commuting miles. Every little bit helps when we go into retirement.

10. Document your information

Keep a list of your contact information so it's easy to find. Each of our clients gets a binder that has a copy of basically all the paperwork that he or she has ever filled out with us. The binder is a good central location to keep important information, including a document for your family and beneficiaries—and for whoever will handle things for you in times of crisis—with contact information for our office and important people involved in your financial affairs. You can keep that binder in a secure place and let your family and other appropriate people know where it can be found.

11. Decide whether to roll funds into an IRA

It's time to decide if you should take the money that is in your 401(k) or 403(b) retirement account and roll it into an IRA. If you're not at your previous employer, your 401(k) shouldn't be there either. Usually, there are better, less expensive options available with an IRA than what you have with a 401(k), but it is a decision that you have to make.

12. Review your Social Security statements

You should examine your Social Security statements to ensure that the reported income is accurate. Sometimes, not all of the income gets reported to the Social Security office. So start taking a look at that—and it's best to do so several years before you'll be getting the money. If the figures are not accurate, contact the Social Security office and find out what type of documentation that it will need to increase the amount of the benefit that you will be paid.

13. Decide when to apply for Social Security

This is a question that we get asked frequently. Determine whether you are going to receive your Social Security benefit early or whether you are going to wait until full retirement age. Again, this can be a tricky and complex question. Sometimes we'll recommend that people do take it early, at sixty-two, especially if you're not going to be working and drawing any income. However, if you're still working and you're planning on retiring at sixty-five or sixty-six, then it probably doesn't make sense to take it early because you're restricted on how much pay you can earn before you have to start giving some of the Social Security income back to the government. Each situation will be a little bit different.

14. Find out what you'll pay for health-care coverage

If you're retiring before you can go on Medicare, then you need to figure out how are you going to handle the time without health insurance or if you will have to pay for an individual policy out-of- pocket. Over the course of your retirement, be prepared to spend hundreds of thousands of dollars. You need to see what your health insurance covers and what you may need to put aside for additional health care costs. The cost of coverage isn't going down. Your doctor's fees are not going down. It's quite the opposite.

We have a lot of clients who would like to retire early but they continue to work strictly for the health insurance. They can't get coverage on their own, perhaps because the premiums are so high, or perhaps because of a pre-existing health condition.

15. Decide on your Medicare coverage options

Just because Medicare plans are alphabetized from A to D, don't be fooled into thinking there are only a few options to consider. Unfortunately deciding which options are right for you isn't as easy as answering a multiple-choice question with one right answer. Everyone's situation is different, and we can help you sort things out.

16. Be aware of required distributions

Once you turn age seventy years, six months, you generally will be required to begin withdrawals from your IRA or 401(k), and you should understand the tax burden associated with it. Often, retirees could just as well live off their pension income and Social Security and don't need the money in their 401(k) or IRA immediately. They may hope that they will not need to touch it until many years into their retirement.

However, when you have a qualified retirement plan, you have to take what's called a required minimum distribution, or RMD, starting at age seventy years, six months. How much depends on your age and the amount in your account at the end of the previous year, but a ballpark amountthat you can plan on having to withdraw is 3.5 percent, and the percentage increases slightly each year.

When you take that required minimum distribution, that's a taxable event. A question I'm often asked is whether you can turn right around and reinvest it in an IRA and get the deduction. Unfortunately, the government does not allow that. It wants its tax revenue. So you have to take it. If you don't take it, you will pay a 50 percent penalty—so if you were supposed to withdraw $2,000 and you don't, then your penalty is going to be $1,000. You don't want to make the mistake of not withdrawing it. How much will the withdrawals affect your overall taxes? We can do calculations to project the RMDs.

17. Be sure your income can survive inflation

Because inflation can seriously erode your purchasing power, you need to determine whether you will need an income stream beyond your pension, Social Security benefits, and savings. I recently met a couple who retired, each at age sixty, after long corporate careers. Obviously they planned well. They're living the American dream. But in these days of medical advances and increased longevity, people need to plan for a twenty-five to thirty-five-year retirement, perhaps even longer. We can run projections, based on your lifestyle needs, to help you determine whether your pension and Social Security income will be enough to last at least to age one-hundred, or longer if you would like.

18. Update your wills and estate plan

I cannot overemphasize the importance of estate planning. Make sure, for example, that you have arranged for a power of attorney in case you are incapacitated. We see it all too often: A client has a stroke or other medical crisis and no longer can write checks or call to withdraw money. You want to make sure somebody you trust will be able to do that on your behalf.

Double check that the beneficiaries are updated on your retirement account. You may want to change the listed beneficiary, for whatever reason—a belief that person is unable to handle money wisely, or concern over a divorce.

Today you may find your adult children's problems bumping into your money, so to speak. It's happening a lot: A child lost a job or went through a divorce and lost half the 401(k), or the house was under water. Adult children in their twenties can't find a job, and in their thirties and forties are in some cases moving back home just as their parents are planning to retire—or else the parents (and sometimes grandparents) are giving them money regularly to care for their kids or stay in school. When we go through the retirement planning analysis, we'll ask clients whether they anticipate any such situation. A good time to consider such questions is when you are updating your wills or trusts.

19. Evaluate your need for long-term-care insurance

The earlier you plan for long-term-care insurance, the more likely that you're going to get it at a reasonable price. People's needs vary, but one rule of thumb is that if you have more than $250,000 in liquid assets and less than $2,000,000 of liquid assets (not total net worth), you need to consider getting long-term-care insurance. If you have less than $250,000 of liquid assets, the premiums are probably going to be more than what you want to bear. And if you have little to no liquid assets when you retire and you're just going to live on fixed income like Social Security, chances are the government's going to take care of you if you need the care. On the other hand, if you have more than $2,000,000 worth of liquid assets, then you are in a financial position where you could self-insure. If you need to go into a nursing home or your spouse needs daily care in the house, you might be able to pay that expense out of pocket, if you have planned well enough.

We have clients who have more than $2,000,000 in liquid assets and still get long-term-care insurance. They could self-insure but choose not to do so, believing it's a better deal to have coverage in place if there should be a claim.

You need to consider your health, the longevity of your parents and other family members, and whether you have a family history of strokes, breast cancer, Alzheimer's or other conditions. Those considerations really determine your need for long-term-care insurance. This is not a fun subject to talk about, but it is a critical area of your retirement plan.

One thing we know for sure is that life is going to throw us curveballs. Your retirement plan can seem sound and work perfectly, and then along comes trouble and the plan isn't worth the paper it is printed on. The one thing that can destroy a lifetime of careful investment and planning is the need for long-term care. Depending on the facility, prices are ranging from sixty to eighty-thousand dollars per year. If you need to have someone come into your house, it's a little less expensive than that, but not a lot. That could still run forty to sixty-thousand dollars per year. That can eat into a retirement nest egg pretty quickly, on top of all the other demands on your money.

When we design a retirement plan, we want to make sure that it is going to work no matter what. Things will not go exactly according to plan during what could be several decades of retirement, but we can anticipate all those contingencies. We can keep risk and volatility low. We can keep fees low. We can generate a reasonable rate of return for our clients.

We have specialists in the office who can help to make sure that your retirement plan is basically bullet-proof—whether you live to an advanced age, or need long-term care, or want to financially support a grandchild who is ill, or whatever situation you might imagine. It's not good enough to have a plan that works only if everything goes perfectly.

20. Enjoy the rest of your life

Go out, celebrate! You've done it. You've made it. You've strived to live the American dream. You got your little piece of the kingdom, so for now go out and enjoy what you worked so hard to attain. We all need to find a balance in our finances, but in the end, that's what money is for: It's to spend and enjoy.

About the Author

Matthew J. Dicken is the founder and CEO of Strategic Wealth Designers. A native of Louisville, KY, Matt attended Ballard High School, obtained his securities licenses at age 18 and began serving the Kentuckiana investment community in 1997.

Since getting his start he has helped thousands of clients realize their retirement goals and dreams. He is a nationally recognized financial educator, counselor to other advisors and contributor to local and national news programs and publications. In his free time Matt enjoys spending time with his wife, Colleen, and their son Winston. They are active supporters of the Animal Care Society, the Make a Wish Foundation and the Wounded Warrior Project. Matt is also a race car enthusiast and lead driver of the Strategic Wealth Racing team.

In 2002 Matt founded Strategic Wealth Designers, a full-service financial planning firm working to help retirees and pre-retirees secure their financial futures. Over the years the firm has experienced tremendous growth and now has offices in Lexington, KY, Indianapolis, IN, Cincinnati, OH and Denver, CO. Thousands of people attend their educational events each year.

Strategic Wealth Designers
National Headquarters 500
North Hurstbourne Parkway
Suite 120
Louisville, Kentucky 40222

Office: 502-412-3354 9710
Fax: 502-327-8566
Toll free: 87-SWD-GROUP
(877-934-7687)

SWDgroup.com

4600 South Syracuse Suite 100
Denver, CO 80237
303-952-4044

5181 Natorp Blvd. Suite 100
Mason, OH 45040
513-492-2918

2716 Old Rosebud Rd. Suite 180
Lexington, KY 40509
859-207-1501

2680 E. Main Street
Plainfield, IN 46168
317-644-0876

Schroeder School of Business
University of Evansville
1800 Lincoln Avenue
Evansville, IN 47722

Celebrating with our client events and SWD Cares charity events.

STRATEGIC WEALTH Cares

Wine Wisdom

FIGHTING
HUNGER!
AT HOME
VOL
UNT
EER

32

Your Retirement Headquarters

Other Ways To Use This Book

Motivate
Educate
Thank
Inspire
Promote Connect

- Build personal bonds with customers, prospects, employees, donors, and key constituencies
- Develop a long-lasting reminder of your event, milestone, or celebration
- Provide a keepsake that inspires change in behavior and change in lives
- Deliver the ultimate "thank you" gift that remains on coffee tables and bookshelves
- Generate the "wow" factor

Books are thoughtful gifts that provide a genuine sentiment that other promotional items cannot express. They promote employee discussions and interaction, rein-force an event's meaning or location, and they make a lasting impression. Use your book to say, "Thank You" and show people that you care.